Portage into the Past

The Fesler-Lampert *Minnesota Heritage* Book Series

This series is published with the generous assistance of
the John K. and Elsie Lampert Fesler Fund and David R. and
Elizabeth P. Fesler. Its mission is to republish significant
out-of-print books that contribute to our understanding and
appreciation of Minnesota and the Upper Midwest.

*Portage into the Past: By Canoe along the Minnesota-Ontario
Boundary Waters* by J. Arnold Bolz

The Gift of the Deer by Helen Hoover

The Long-Shadowed Forest by Helen Hoover

A Place in the Woods by Helen Hoover

The Years of the Forest by Helen Hoover

North Star Country by Meridel Le Sueur

Listening Point by Sigurd F. Olson

The Lonely Land by Sigurd F. Olson

Of Time and Place by Sigurd F. Olson

Open Horizons by Sigurd F. Olson

Reflections from the North Country by Sigurd F. Olson

Runes of the North by Sigurd F. Olson

The Singing Wilderness by Sigurd F. Olson

Voyageur Country: The Story of Minnesota's National Park
by Robert Treuer

J. ARNOLD BOLZ

Portage into the Past

By Canoe along the Minnesota-Ontario Boundary Waters

ILLUSTRATIONS BY
FRANCIS LEE JAQUES

University of
Minnesota Press
MINNEAPOLIS
LONDON

Published by the University of Minnesota Press
111 Third Avenue South, Suite 290
Minneapolis, MN 55401-2520
http://www.upress.umn.edu

Printed in the United States of America on acid-free paper

Library of Congress Cataloging-in-Publication Data
Bolz, J. Arnold.
Portage into the past : by canoe along the Minnesota-Ontario
boundary waters / J. Arnold Bolz ; illustrations by Francis Lee Jaques.
p.   cm. — (The Fesler-Lampert Minnesota heritage book series)
Originally published: 1960.
Includes bibliographical references and index.
ISBN 0-8166-0919-5
1. Boundary Waters Canoe Area (Minn.)—Description and travel.
2. Bolz, J. Arnold—Journeys—Minnesota.   3. Bolz, J. Arnold—
Journeys—Ontario.   4. Canoes and canoeing—Minnesota.   5. Canoes and
canoeing—Ontario.   6. Natural History—Minnesota—Boundary Waters
Canoe Area.   7. Superior National Forest Region (Minn.)—Description
and travel.   8. Quetico Provincial Park Region (Ont.)—Description
and travel.   I. Title.   II. Series.
F612.B73B65   1999
917.76'7—dc21   99-13545

The University of Minnesota is an equal-opportunity
educator and employer.

11 10 09 08 07 06 05 04 03 02 01 00 99   10 9 8 7 6 5 4 3 2 1

FOR MY

femme du nord

WHOSE ENTHUSIASM FOR THE
QUETICO-SUPERIOR COUNTRY EQUALS MINE
AND WHOSE HELP WITH THIS
BOOK AFFIRMED IT

Table of Contents

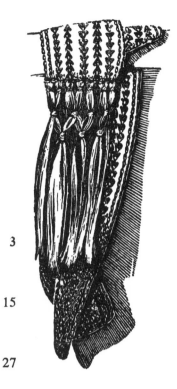

PROLOGUE   3

December 27, 1957. CRANE LAKE, MINNESOTA, NORTHWEST OF DULUTH, IN THE MINNESOTA-ONTARIO BORDER COUNTRY   15

October 1, 1958. GRAND PORTAGE, MINNESOTA, AT THE MOST NORTHEASTERN TIP OF MINNESOTA, ON LAKE SUPERIOR   27

Sketch Map for October 1–5, *page 31*

October 2. ON THE GRAND PORTAGE TRAIL FROM LAKE SUPERIOR TO FORT CHARLOTTE ON THE PIGEON RIVER   48

October 3. FORT CHARLOTTE TO THE MEADOW ON THE PIGEON RIVER   54

October 4. FROM THE MEADOW TO MOUNTAIN LAKE   62

October 5. MOUNTAIN LAKE TO ROSE LAKE   72

October 6. ROSE LAKE TO LAKE SAGANAGA   78

October 7. LAKE SAGANAGA TO CYPRESS LAKE   86

Sketch Map for October 6–10, *page 90*

October 8. CYPRESS LAKE TO BASSWOOD LAKE   97

October 9. BASSWOOD LAKE TO CROOKED LAKE   107

October 10. CROOKED LAKE TO LAC LA CROIX   121

Sketch Map for October 11, *page 134*

October 11. LAC LA CROIX TO BARE PORTAGE ON
NAMAKAN LAKE   130

BIBLIOGRAPHY   173

INDEX   175

Contemporary Scenes, *between pages 88 and 89*

"Lake Superior" by Frances Ann Hopkins

"Shooting the Rapids" by Frances Ann Hopkins

"Bivouac of Canoe Party" by Frances Ann Hopkins

"Canoe Party around a Campfire" by Frances Ann Hopkins

Upper Basswood Falls, an illustration from John Bigsby's *The Shoe and Canoe*, 1850

"Canoe Proceeding along High Rocky Cliffs" by Frances Ann Hopkins

Lac La Croix, an illustration from John Bigsby's *The Shoe and Canoe*, 1850

Sir George Simpson, Hudson's Bay Company Governor, on an inspection tour

The map on the endpapers is adapted from the "Plan Shewing the Region Explored by S. J. Dawson and His Party between Fort William, Lake Superior, and the Great Saskatchewan River from 1st of August 1857, to 1st of November 1858"

PORTAGE INTO THE PAST

Prologue

LYING astride the boundary between Minnesota and Ontario is the Quetico-Superior canoe country. Here, in the boundless freedom of the wilderness, is a wondrous maze of sparkling lakes and streams. Pine, aspen, and birch cover the rock of the Canadian shield with a mantle of green. Bears, moose, and deer roam the forest. Beavers build their dams, fish swirl in the blue waters, and loons fill the air with laughter.

Still primitive and wild, the Quetico-Superior may appear to be without a history. Yet it has a long one, rich in adventure and romance. As an integral part of a great internal system of waterways — the St. Lawrence–Lake Superior route to the Northwest — it occupied an important position in the early history of the continent. For two hundred and fifty years, colorful adventurers used its lakes and streams as highways to the *pays d'en haut*, the upper country.

Transported in frail bark canoes paddled by French-Canadian voyageurs, some went to find a passage to the riches of the Orient, others to exploit the wealth of furs in the Northwest, still others to build a nation.

Starting in the late 1600's and continuing for nearly a century, a tide of spirited Frenchmen ebbed and flowed along the western shores of Lake Superior. Leaving Montreal, the sons of New France carried the fleur-de-lis over the clear waters of the inland sea and pushed further into the interior. There were black-robed Jesuit missionaries with crucifixes to save Indian souls for the greater glory of God, bold explorers with swords flashing in the sun to search for the Western Sea and to claim vast areas of land for the greater glory of the king, and fur traders with packs seeking to exchange goods and trinkets for peltries with the Indians for the greater glory of themselves.

Slowly spreading west, first through the Kaministikwia waterway and later through Grand Portage, the French finally reached the Missouri River and the Black Hills. At the same time they established a route to the forks of the Saskatchewan River. In the border country they built posts at Grand Portage, Lake Saganaga, Basswood Lake, Crane Lake, Rainy River, and Lake of the Woods. Although the Western Sea eluded them, the route through the Quetico-Superior enabled them to intercept Indian trade passing over waterways leading to the English on Hudson's Bay. It also led to rich beaver lands in the Northwest, relieving the difficulties of competition with English traders to the south.

While thus engaged, the French slowly developed the basic features of the fur trade — the barter and credit system, the use of the French language, the necessity of licenses for regulation, the establishment of forts and military posts for protection, the best routes to follow in reaching the beaver lands, and, above all, the employment of voyageurs, without whose services the whole venture would not have been possible; all these features were to continue as long as the fur trade flourished.

In 1763, France lost its colony to England. Soon after, English, Scotch, and Yankee traders from Montreal replaced the French, as they in turn sought the wealth of the interior. Although temporarily discouraged by a general Indian uprising under Pontiac, they began to flood the Northwest, first through Grand Portage and then, after 1804, over the Kaministikwia route. The change to the Kaministikwia was made necessary when Grand Portage became United States territory after the American Revolution.

Individually, these men continued the trading methods of the French. But, unlike the French, they were free from government intervention.

4

Rum began to flow in ever-increasing amounts. Violence and bloodshed followed underbidding, with consequent loss of profits. Excessive competition among the traders and the Montreal merchants' fear of non-issuance of licenses to trade (this was the period of the American Revolution and the governor was apprehensive about trade goods' falling into the hands of the rebelling colonists) led to a pooling of interests in 1780, and, four years later, to the formation of an association of the traders without charter or monopoly rights, the famous North West Company.

Of the Nor'Westers, most of whom were Scottish Highlanders, W. Stewart Wallace wrote: "these men were hardy, courageous, shrewd, and proud. They spent a good part of their lives traveling incredible distances in birch-bark canoes, shooting rapids, or navigating inland seas. They were wrecked and drowned. They suffered hunger and starvation. They were robbed and murdered by the Indians, and sometimes by one another. They fell the victims of small pox, syphilis, and rum."

Under the leadership of two Montreal merchants, first Simon McTavish and later William McGillivray, they built an empire that extended over half of the continent. Daring and ruthless, the "Master Pedlars," as they were called by the Hudson's Bay Company traders, followed the waterways through the Quetico-Superior to continue the search for the Western Sea and greatly expand the fur trade.

In so doing they intercepted the flow of Indian trade to the Hudson's Bay Company, as the French had done before them. The Hudson's Bay Company had been chartered by King Charles II of England in 1670 through the machinations of Pierre Radisson and given exclusive trading rights in Hudson's Bay and its drainage basin. Until this time, it had been content to remain on the bay, waiting for the Indians to bring furs to it. Now, roused from its lethargy, the company began to penetrate the interior in active competition with the North West Company. A bitter struggle ensued — actually a contest over whether Hudson's Bay or the St. Lawrence was the better approach to the furs of the north.

During the years 1812–1821, the struggle reached its climax. In 1812 Lord Selkirk, a visionary colonizer and chief stockholder of the Hudson's Bay Company, halted the flood of Nor'Westers by building a dike, in the form of the Red River settlements, across the North West Company's supply lines already overextended from Montreal through the Quetico-Superior to the Arctic Circle and the Pacific slopes. These lines were supplied by pemmican — pounded dried buffalo meat — which the Nor'Westers obtained yearly from the Indians and then stored at Fort Gibraltar on the Red River.

After the founding of the settlements, the Quetico-Superior region saw the comings and goings of the participants in the North West Company's struggle for survival as they traveled to and from the major area of strife — the Red River settlements. In the successive conflicts between the North West Company and Selkirk's colony, counterarrest followed arrest as the seizure of forts and pemmican supplies provoked counterseizure and bloodshed. Arrested officials and discouraged settlers of the colony were taken east over boundary waters in the canoes of the victorious North West Company. To halt the Nor'Westers, Lord Selkirk himself appeared in 1816, capturing Fort William, the rendezvous of the North West Company. In order to get provisions for the winter, he sent a group of one hundred voyageurs and one hundred Swiss de Meuron mercenaries, equipped with two field pieces, over the Kaministikwia to capture the North West Company post on the Rainy River. In the spring, he proceeded to the Red River to reorganize his dwindling colony.

The boundary itself was involved in the struggle. When John McKay, in 1793, erected a Hudson's Bay Company fort on the Rainy River near Manitou Rapids, the contest began; it continued until the post was abandoned in 1797. Competition from the Nor'Westers, who had long occupied the area with posts at Grand Portage, Crane Lake, and Rainy River, proved too much for the new post. Again in 1818, however, with the Nor'Westers weakened from the general struggle, the Hudson's Bay Company built a post on the Rainy River, this time just below the falls at the outlet of the lake. Built by Robert Dickson, the fort was a success, later becoming the city of Fort Frances. Subsidiary posts followed in the Quetico-Superior on Moose, Basswood, and Crane Lakes.

The competitors grew to three when the American Fur Company bought the posts of the North West Company at the headwaters of the Mississippi. For many years, the Nor'Westers had illegally maintained these posts south of the present boundary. British title to this land had terminated at the

The Quetico-Superior canoe country (the heavy broken line is the U.S.-Canadian border; R.A. marks roadless areas)

Treaty of Peace in 1783 following the American Revolution, and again at the Treaty of Ghent after the War of 1812. Nevertheless, the North West Company continued to fly the Union Jack from their posts in Minnesota, until 1816, when Congress prohibited foreigners from trading with Indians on United States soil. This bill, passed largely as a result of the persuasions of John Jacob Astor, allowed the American Fur Company, which he had founded in 1808, to gain a foothold in the area. Not long after, the Hudson's Bay Company lashed out at the newly purchased American Fur Company posts, sending fifty of its men into United States territory to disrupt the trade of American's Fond du Lac department.

Finally exhausted from the struggle, the North West Company could no longer continue. Burdened with overextended supply lines, strained finances, and disrupted trade, it sought negotiation with the Hudson's Bay Company, also weakened from the struggle. The meetings which followed in London ended in victory for the Hudson's Bay Company and union of the two companies in 1821.

After the union, York Factory on Hudson's Bay replaced Montreal as the fur capital. The York Factory–Fort Garry (Winnipeg) passage then replaced the long and costly haul that the Nor'Westers had had to make

7

from Montreal to the interior. Traffic over the Kaministikwia dropped to a trickle, consisting primarily of Hudson's Bay Company officers housed in Montreal.

Even though the North West Company no longer existed, fur-trading activity continued in the Quetico-Superior. Until the mid-nineteenth century, Hudson's Bay Company traders passed eastward from Rainy Lake to their posts scattered through the border country. In addition to their own traders, the Hudson's Bay Company licensed Red River métis to obtain furs for them across the border. These métis, or half-breeds, had free access to both sides of the boundary because of their Indian blood. From 1822 to 1833, traders of the American Fur Company appeared on border waters from Fond du Lac to their posts at Grand Portage, Moose Lake, Basswood Lake, and Rainy River. Besides these, there were always a few independent traders.

In 1833 the American Fur Company gave up its posts when John Jacob Astor, realizing that his fortunes lay westward along the trail of Lewis and Clark, agreed, for an annual payment of three hundred pounds sterling, to stop its relentless competition with the Hudson's Bay Company.

By mid-century, after laying open the wilderness, the fur trade began to recede as the pressures of civilization increased. Earlier, civilization's vanguard had slowly begun to appear from along the St. Lawrence. Over the ensuing years, naturalists, geologists, artists, engineers, soldiers, missionaries, sportsmen, immigrants, and an occasional dauntless woman followed the Kaministikwia "road" through the Quetico-Superior on their way to the West. They continued using this "road," as these wilderness waterways and portages were then known, until dirt roads with carts and stagecoaches and finally, in the 1880's, the Canadian Pacific Railway replaced the waterways, which passed into history along with the red-capped voyageurs and bark canoes.

With civilization advancing westward, the Kaministikwia route again assumed importance, this time reaching its greatest usefulness in the decade following 1870, as part of an all-Canadian route to the West — the Dawson Road.

The chain of events which led to the building of this Road started in 1857. In that year, the Canadian government, as a part of its plans to hold the British West against the territorial aggressiveness of American pioneers, sent Henry Hind, a geologist and naturalist, and Simon Dawson, a surveyor and engineer, to explore the Northwest, especially the region between Lake Superior and the Red River settlements. The purpose of the expedition was twofold: to find an all-Canadian route west to speed migration and to investigate the territorial claims of Canada in opposition to those of the Hudson's Bay Company, whose control over the territory granted them in the charter from King Charles II was about to expire. In the same year, the British government sent an expedition under Captain John Palliser with the same twofold purpose as the Canadian expedition under Hind and Dawson.

Both expeditions kept full accounts of their travels, including reports on the area's flora, fauna, geology, Indians, missions, settlements, and fur trade. Palliser reported that the Kaministikwia was impracticable as an approach to the West, while Dawson, more optimistic about crossing the wilderness barrier from Lake Superior to the Red River, recommended that the Kaministikwia be used as part of the route west.

Dawson's ideas were followed, but progress in carrying out his plans was slow. In 1868, the Canadian government began work on roads from the Northwest Angle to Fort Garry, and from Port Arthur fifty miles west to Lake Shebandowan.

In 1870 the Dawson Road became a reality, because in that year the métis at the Red River settlements, under the leadership of Louis Riel, began an armed rebellion to prevent the loss of their squatter's rights in the transfer of much of the Hudson's Bay Company territory to Canada. To quell the rebellion, the Canadian government sent an expeditionary force of fourteen hundred men, under the brilliant leadership of Colonel Garnet Wolseley, from Toronto to Fort Garry. Leaving Prince Arthur's Landing, now Port Arthur, on July 1, the soldiers arrived at Fort Garry on August 24, disappointed to find the half-breeds disbanded. But they had accomplished something; for, en route over the Kaministikwia, they actually built the road that Dawson had surveyed through the wilderness. They had cleared the road of trees and rocks, erected bridges, and built blockhouses to serve as commissaries.

Now the Canadian government supported the building of the road as

Dawson had envisaged it, for its value as a link between East and West was becoming more obvious. Steamboats were launched on Sturgeon Lake, Lac la Croix, Rainy Lake, and other large bodies of water. Dams were erected, raising the water level over difficult stretches and thus making them navigable for steam tugs. The portages were covered with corduroy and supplied with carts. An occasional overnight hostelry was erected to accommodate the expected flow of immigrants.

Although used by numerous immigrants, traders, and other travelers, the road was never a success. It was a rugged, five-hundred-mile journey through the wilderness, involving seventeen changes. Transfers were made into steamboats, carts, York boats, canoes, steam tugs, and stagecoaches. It was so arduous that many travelers preferred a rival route through Minnesota, via St. Paul and the Red River trails. This Minnesota route, with its greater capacity and economy, had already supplanted the York Factory approach to the Northwest. It led, fifteen hundred miles in all, from Montreal to Chicago by steamer, to St. Paul by rail, to Breckenridge by stagecoach, and to Fort Garry by sternwheeler on the Red River. Even though the route through Minnesota was easier, the all-Canadian Dawson Road through the Quetico-Superior nevertheless remained in use for a decade.

So men came and went, exploring, trading, and bringing civilization. France, England, and the United States at various times laid claim to the Quetico-Superior. Diplomats drew arbitrary boundary lines through it, finally settling on a line in 1842. The area south of this line became part of the newly formed state of Minnesota in 1858, while the area north of the line became a part of the Dominion of Canada when confederation took place in 1867. Yet the Quetico-Superior itself remained virtually unchanged, retaining its wild, primeval beauty.

Many of the adventurers through the Quetico-Superior kept journals, varying in language from the quaint phonetic spelling of Peter Pond and the stilted Old World prose of Sir Alexander Mackenzie to the polished writing of the Reverend George Grant. Through their worn pages, the modern voyageur may penetrate the north country and partake of the freedom, pleasures, adventures, mishaps, and dangers of its early travelers. Paddling over its lakes, packing across its portages, and camping on early

10

campsites, he will join this great company. And in reading these accounts he will gain a feeling of intimacy with the past. He will learn of the mystery in the names Basswood and Lac la Croix, and the meaning of Saganaga and Gunflint. He will glimpse the country as man first knew it. In the process he will develop a greater appreciation of the wilderness area and its heritage.

THE JOURNAL

December 27, 1957. CRANE LAKE, MINNESOTA, NORTH-
WEST OF DULUTH, IN THE MINNESOTA-ONTARIO BORDER COUNTRY

THROUGH the blurring whiteness of the December storm, the pines stood rigid against the onslaught of the chill north wind that swirled the snow in gusts around the corners of the cabin and piled drifts along the banks of the Echo River. Inside the cabin, the fire thrust orange spears from the logs in the fireplace; it spat sparks of defiance up the chimney while throwing cheerful warmth into the room. I sat before it, reading a diary written long ago by an early traveler on his way through this same Quetico-Superior canoe country.

The groaning of cabin logs shrinking from the cold outside distracted me, and as I looked up, several chickadees, eager to fortify themselves against the cold, flew into the feeders just outside the window. They announced with a gleeful chorus of *chicka-dee-dee* the arrival of my wife,

Belva, and her parents, Millie and John Nelson; for just then they pushed open the door and, accompanied by a flurry of cold air, came in stamping their feet and brushing off snow. They had been snowshoeing through the white forest near the cabin in search of Millie's pet deer, which had not been in to feed for the past two days.

Millie exclaimed as she pulled off a mitten, "This is the night hell's going to freeze over!"

John snorted, pushed his fogged glasses up on his forehead, then walked over to the frosted window to peer at the thermometer outside, "Yup, it's twenty below already."

"Did you find the deer?" I asked.

Belva pointed out the window. "Look!"

I looked out to see the year-old doe solemnly munching alfalfa as she stared at us through the window.

"She was right where I thought she'd be, out in the cedar swamp," said Millie, as she pulled off the other mitten, parka, and boots before easing herself down on her favorite stool, backside to the fire.

"What on earth is that old book you're reading, Arnold?" she inquired.

"It's a copy of Hind's *Exploring Expeditions*," Belva answered for me. "I love those old books. They even smell exciting!"

"Who's he?" asked John, stopping to glance over my shoulder as he brought me a cup of hot coffee — the royal kind, I was pleased to find.

"In 1857, the Canadian government sent Henry Hind, a surveyor, and Simon Dawson, a geologist, to find an all-Canadian route west of Lake Superior to the Red River settlements, at what is now Winnipeg," I explained.

"You mean our Dawson Portage Dawson?" Millie asked.

"Yes," I answered. "Do you remember the times you've camped at Snake Falls on the Namakan River?"

Millie nodded. "Sure, what about it?"

"When you came in, I was reading what Hind had written as he camped there over a hundred years ago."

"Let's hear it," said John.

I flipped back a page.

"The dawn of morning and the early start in this rocky wilderness pos-

16

sess some characteristics peculiar to the country and the strange companions with whom necessity compels you to associate. Rising from a bed on the hard rock, which you have softened by a couple of rugs or a north blanket, and if time and opportunity permitted by fresh spruce or pine boughs, the aspect of the sky first claims and almost invariably receives attention. The morning is probably calm, the stars are slightly paling, cold yellow light begins to show itself in the east; on the river or lake rests a screen of dense fog, landwards a wall of forest inpenetrable to the eye. Walking a step or two from the camp a sudden rush through the underbrush tells of a fox, mink, or marten prowling close by, probably attracted by the remains of last night's meal. From the dying camp fires a thin column of smoke rises high above the trees, or spreads lakewards to join the damp misty veil which hides the quiet waters from view. Around the fires are silent forms like shrouded corpses stretched at full length on the bare rock or on spruce branches carefully arranged. These are the Indians, they have completely enveloped themselves in their blankets, and lie motionless on their backs. Beneath upturned canoes, or lying like the Indians, with their feet to the fire, the French voyageurs are found scattered about the camp; generally the servant attached to each tent stretches himself before the canvas door. No sound at this season of the year disturbs the silence of the early dawn if the night has been cold and calm. The dull music of a distant waterfall is sometimes heard, or its unceasing roar when camped close to it as on the Rattlesnake Portage, but these are exceptional cases, in general all nature seems sunk in perfect repose, and the silence is almost oppressive. As the dawn advances an Indian awakes, uncovers his face, sits on his haunches and looks around from beneath the folds of his blanket which he has drawn over his head. After a few minutes have thus passed, not observing his companions show any sign of waking or disposition to rise, he utters a low 'waugh'; slowly other forms unroll themselves, sit on their haunches and look around in silence. Three or four minutes are allowed to pass away when one of them rises and arranges the fire, adding fresh wood and blowing the embers into a flame. He calls a French voyageur by name, who leaps from his couch, and in a low voice utters 'lève, lève.' Two or three of his companions quickly rise, remain for a few minutes on their knees in prayer, and then shout lustily 'lève, messieurs, lève.' In another minute all is life, the motionless forms under the canoes, by the camp fires, under trees, or stretched before the tent doors, spring to their feet. The canvas is shaken and ten minutes given to dress, the tent pins are then unloosened and the half dressed laggard rushes into the open air to escape the damp folds of the tent now threatening to envelope him. Meanwhile the canoes are launched and the baggage stowed away. The voyageurs and travellers take their seats, a hasty look is thrown around to see that no stray frying pan or hatchet is left behind, and the start is made. An effort to be cheerful and sprightly is soon damped by the mist in which we plunge, and no sound but the measured stroke of the paddle greets the ear. The sun begins to glimmer above the horizon, the fog clears slowly away, a loon or a flock of ducks fly wildly across the bow of the first canoe, the Indians and voyageurs shout at the frightened birds or imitate their cry with admirable accuracy, the guide stops, pipes are lit, and a cheerful day is begun."

Millie turned and stared thoughtfully into the fire. "You know, they might possibly have picked the same spot for their tent as we did. I can just see them there."

John took the book from me and asked, "Where did you get this?"

Belva explained, "You remember how lonesome Arnold and I were for the border lakes those two years we spent in the army in Colorado? We read and reread Florence Jaques' *Canoe Country* and it was the next best thing to being there. She quotes snatches from the diaries of explorers and fur traders, and we began wondering if any of the diaries might still be available. So Arnold went snooping in bookstores until he found a dealer who said he'd try to find some of the diaries we wanted. He couldn't promise, because they were darned hard to find."

"What happened?" Millie inquired.

"We waited and waited. It seemed like ages, though it was really only a few weeks. When the first package came from Wright Howes, a rare book dealer in Chicago, we tore it open like a couple of kids and found two gorgeous old leather books. Their covers were smooth and soft, with beautiful gold leaf tooling. On the backs it said *The Shoe and Canoe*, Bigsby. The name seemed as enticing as the books turned out to be. Doesn't that one smell old and intriguing? Look where it was printed — in London.

18

Most of them were. The canoe country was important in Europe in those days."

John felt, sniffed at the leather, then opened the old book.

Belva went on. "After that, as each book came, we'd eagerly turn its fragile pages to the part that told of the border lakes. Then we'd search for descriptions of how the country looked, what names had been used then for the lakes and portages, where a fur post might have been, or what experiences the diarist had. We learned about the voyageurs too. It was all fascinating!"

John broke in, "How many of these old books do you have now?"

"Most of them, I think. About thirty," I answered. "They came from Wright Howes, Goodspeed's in Boston, Peter Decker in New York, and Ross and Haines in Minneapolis. We have others, of course, that deal with fur trade and exploration — mostly histories. But the diaries are much more interesting because they were written by the people who actually made the history."

John thumbed through the book. "Huh, I realized that a lot had happened here; but I didn't know so much of it had been written down."

"Say, Arnold," Millie got up to move her stool further from the fire, "after you've read these old books, I should think you and Belva would take that trip you've been talking about the last few years."

"You mean from Grand Portage to Rainy Lake?" I asked. "Oh, I don't know. We'll do it sometime, maybe."

"There's only one way to do anything like that," John said firmly, as he went to get more coffee. "Set a date far enough ahead, then do it."

"Do it next summer," Millie suggested.

"I think that's a wonderful idea, Arnold," Belva said enthusiastically. "Now that we've read so much and the details are so real to us, it would be a perfect time to follow the voyageurs' route."

"Now, just wait a minute," John objected. "You'd want Harvi as a guide, so you would have to go sometime when he's not busy guiding for the resort. You'd better go in October. He'd be free then."

"To heck with Harvi, I'll go. Wouldn't that be fun?" Millie asked hopefully.

"That's what you think. We want help, not hindrance," Belva laughed.

19

"October would be a good time to go — warm days, cool nights, lots of color, and no mosquitoes."

"Do you suppose Harvi would go?" I wondered.

Harvi, a guide in the Quetico-Superior and long a friend, had always been our *homme du nord*, or man of the north, on our trips into the canoe country. Adept and knowledgeable in the art of wilderness travel, he always imparted a feeling of security in the wilds.

"The only way to find out is to ask him," John answered.

"Look, another deer!" Millie exclaimed, pointing out the window.

White flag erect, a buck bounded in great leaps across the ice on the river, and then disappeared into the shadows of the forest.

The wind had stopped and the sky was almost clear. The sun was descending, leaving a trail of small clouds like pink lambs' tails in the west. The snowdrifts momentarily held a golden sheen, then mauve shadows moved quickly over them.

After dinner, I decided to talk to Harvi about the trip.

As I walked briskly along in the below-zero night, my breath condensed and hung about my head. The white moon peered, cold and unyielding, from behind columns of black Norways. Its light chased purple shadows out of hiding and stretched them across the glittering snow. No sound disturbed the silent forest except the quick crunch, crunch, crunch of snow under my feet.

Rounding a bend in the road, I could see smoke feathering upwards through the fir trees that sheltered Harvi's small log cabin. Yellow light, escaping through the windows, reflected on huge icicles that hung from the eaves. They made a gay holiday decoration, twinkling and glittering in the December moonlight. The vagrant trail of a snowshoe rabbit led hophazardly from under the steps and into the evergreen depths close by.

"Come in." A gay feminine voice answered my knock. I entered to find Harvi, his wife Terri, and little Harvi, my friend's pint-sized counterpart, just finishing their supper.

Harvi, an average-sized man, rose and with the slow, easy grace of a woodsman, walked across the room to greet me. He extended his hand, and, as usual, said, "Hi, Doc. How are things?" Then he stepped back, as I entered, and shut the door. He scratched his head and broke into a

20

disconcerting leprechaun grin, which, with his ski-slide nose, gave to his otherwise stolid Finnish countenance a slightly rakish appearance.

As we settled ourselves near the barrel stove to catch more of its warmth, I answered, "Fine. How's the trapline?"

"It's gone pretty well so far. Just covered ten or twelve miles of it this morning. Got a wolf and fox this time."

"Where is your trapline this year — same as always?"

Terri excused herself and went to put little Harvi to bed.

"Yeah, about the same, along Echo River to Bayliss and Bug Lakes for rats and mink. Got some traps set along the ridges for wolves and fox, a few in the swamps for bobcats." Harvi continued. "By the way, I found two deer today that had been killed by wolves. Blood and hair and parts of the carcasses were all over the snow."

"Well, Harvi, you can't blame the wolves. It's the same old story — survival of the fittest."

"I suppose that's right."

Harvi got up and beckoned me to follow him to the storeroom, an unheated room which reeked of musk and grease.

"Pew," I complained.

Harvi just laughed. He was used to the smell of untanned skins. Hanging about the room on stretchers were skins of muskrat, mink, fox, fisher, and bobcat. He handed me a mink pelt. "Feel this. Isn't it a beauty?"

The texture of the fur under my hand felt slightly coarse and rough. "This sure feels different from the way *castor gras d'hiver* must have felt."

Harvi turned. "Castor what?"

"*Castor gras d'hiver*," I explained. "That's French for beaver pelts taken when prime in winter. The Indians wore them, fur side next to their skin, before trading. As a result, they lost their guard hairs, and became soft and silky from contact with body oils. They were highly prized by early traders."

"These pelts will get that way too when they're treated," Harvi replied. "Here, feel this beaver blanket I took last spring."

Deep in furs, I thought this was the time to question Harvi about our proposed trip. "Harvi, how would you like to go with Belva and me on a long canoe trip next October?"

A firm believer in the principle of the conservation of energy, Harvi asked first, "How long are the portages?"

"There are only two bad ones. Grand Portage is nine miles long and the New Grand Portage about two and a half miles."

Harvi shook his head, then scratched it thoughtfully.

"Have you got a map around?" I asked. "Let's take a look at it."

We returned to the front room where Harvi pulled a large canoe map of the border country from a high shelf and spread it on the floor.

Kneeling by the map, I traced the route along the boundary west from Grand Portage, across the long mountain-locked lakes to Height of Land, northwest through Gunflint Lake and the Granite River to Saganaga, down through Knife Lake to Basswood, down the rapids of Basswood River to Crooked Lake, from Crooked to Lac la Croix, through the windings of Loon River to Namakan Lake, and from there to Rainy Lake — some two hundred miles of water, about fifteen miles of portages.

Harvi said nothing.

"This was actually only a small part of the waterway the old traders took to the Northwest," I explained, hoping Harvi might not feel the trip was so long after all, by comparison. "By the time they reached Grand Portage they had already paddled eighteen hundred miles from Montreal, and many had two thousand more to go before reaching the Arctic tundra or the Pacific slopes!"

"Seems to me I've heard of another route west of Lake Superior," Harvi grinned. "Wouldn't that be easier?"

"That must be the Kaministikwia route from Fort William. It joined the Grand Portage 'road' through Sturgeon Lake and the Maligne River at Lac la Croix," I replied. "No, it's not easier. The voyageurs had to be coaxed into using it."

"Well, that's out," Harvi quickly replied. Then he slowly gave me the answer I had been waiting for. "Well, Arnold, if you *really* want to go, sure — we'll make 'er somehow."

"I thought I was going to have a harder time convincing you," I said with a sigh of relief. "You can be our voyageur!"

"All right, but I wear my own hat," Harvi stated firmly, as he left to get more wood for the stove.

22

I laughed to myself, as I pictured him in a voyageur's red cap with a flame sash hanging from his waist.

Yet the position of the voyageurs in history was no laughing matter; for without their services the fur trade of the North could not have been carried on, nor could exploration have proceeded as it did.

The voyageurs originated during the French regime from a group of men called *coureurs de bois,* or woodsrunners. The latter group came into existence when the more distant Indians failed to bring their furs to the colony on the St. Lawrence through fear of the Iroquois, who infested nearby waterways. Happily abandoning the tedium of the fields for freedom and adventure in the wilderness, French habitants left their homes to venture inland to get furs. In time it was necessary that licenses be issued to prevent abuses and regulate the trade. The *coureurs de bois* were then hired by the licensed fur merchants or traders to man their canoes and help carry on the trade. Thus, the French-Canadian canoemen, or voyageurs, were born. Later, as the trade became more complex, a division of labor among the voyageurs themselves was necessary.

It was after the period of French rule, during the time when they were employed by the North West Company, and later by the Hudson's Bay Company and the American Fur Company, that the voyageurs' services were of most importance. Certainly more colorful than the Western cowboys, and of far greater significance to the destiny of this continent, the voyageurs have not been accorded their rightful place in history.

Coming from Montreal, Quebec, and smaller towns on the St. Lawrence, most voyageurs preferred their hard wilderness life to any other. In the summer they toiled over rough, mosquito-infested portages with packs of trade goods and furs. They paddled their canoes, forty strokes a minute or faster, sixty to eighty miles a day, from dawn to dusk, over lakes now lashed to a fury by storms, or again shimmering and still in the hot sun. Expertly they guided their craft down treacherous rivers and through boiling rapids. In the winter they spent the short days at wilderness forts, doing their chores, often snowshoeing through white forests and over icebound lakes to trade with the Indians. They labored uncomplainingly, always obedient to the commands of their employers.

Poorly paid though they were, the assurance of a full belly at least once a day, an occasional treat of high wines, brief respites spent in smoking, the joy of handling their canoes, and the pleasurable companionship of the dusky daughters of the forest were enough to keep them happy and singing.

The typical voyageur was a short swarthy man, powerfully built, with the endurance of an ox, yet graceful and lithe as a cat. The earliest voyageur dressed, of necessity, in Indian buckskins. A little later he wore the more practicable cloth of the European, as did the Indian with whom he traded. Though the buckskin breechcloth and thigh-length leggings were soon discarded for pants of blue denim, he always wore moccasins, for he could carry a year's supply of them in his pack. His short red or blue shirt was snugged in at the waist by a gaudy fringed sash from which hung a beaded bag for his tobacco and white clay pipes. In cool weather he added a hooded blue jacket. His *pièce de résistance* was a red wool cap which he wore at a jaunty angle.

He was invariably boastful about his own prowess and ready to ridicule lesser talents, dirty and smelly, profane and immoral, quick to anger, illiterate, superstitious, reckless but not brave, and extremely class-conscious. Nevertheless, he was gentle, kind, and hopelessly romantic; deeply religious, obedient, loyal, and extremely courteous; gay, voluble, effervescent, constantly talking in his expressive French, gesticulating, and singing, full of the lust for life. He was a voyageur, and mighty proud of it!

One of the voyageurs, long past seventy, summed it up this way: "I could carry, paddle, walk and sing with any man I ever saw. I have been twenty-four years a canoeman, and forty-one years in service; no portage was ever too long for me. Fifty songs could I sing. I have saved the life of ten *voyageurs*. Have had twelve wives and six running dogs. I spent all my money in pleasure. Were I young again, I should spend my life the same way over. There is no life so happy as a *voyageur's* life."

Considering all of this, I decided Harvi would not qualify in every respect as a voyageur; he would have to be one in name only. Actually it would have been more fitting to have pictured him in a Viking helmet complete with horns. But even then he could still in a sense qualify as a voyageur; for, when the Vikings visited Normandy long ago, they left traces of blond hair and blue eyes for some of the future voyageurs.

24

When Harvi returned with an armful of logs, he said, "I'll circle the first of October on the calendar. You go ahead and make your plans."

It was late, so I returned home and went to bed, my head filled with thoughts of our trip next fall. This was one of those trips one dreams about for years, without its materializing; then some casual happening makes it a reality, without fuss or fanfare.

I lay planning what we would do next autumn. We would go to Grand Portage on Lake Superior, then follow the customary waterway of the explorers and fur traders through the Quetico-Superior to Rainy Lake.

To feel the presence of early travelers as our companions, we would read during our journey from a notebook into which we had copied our favorite passages from the diaries they had left while traveling in this same area. We would concentrate on those of Dr. John Bigsby and Major Joseph Delafield, for they are more detailed and filled with human interest. The others are short records or daily logs in which few personal experiences are noted. From these last we would take only passages of interest to us.

In 1823 Bigsby and Delafield traveled over border waters as commissioners, attempting to determine the disputed boundary line between Canada and the United States under the Treaty of Ghent in 1814. Delafield was head of the American section of the joint commission. Under his personal direction most of the boundary line between St. Regis on the St. Lawrence and the most northwesterly point of Lake of the Woods was determined. His diaries, published as *The Unfortified Boundary*, were supplementary to his official documents. Bigsby was the assistant secretary to the British commission assigned to the same area. He was accompanied by David Thompson, the famous geographer and Nor'Wester. Included in Bigsby's diary, *The Shoe and Canoe*, are his sketches, our first authentic pictures of the border lakes.

I turned in bed, and through the window Orion was bright in the winter sky. The rock ridge across the river sharply resounded the boom and zing of shifting ice in the river. I thought of Bourassa, one of La Vérendrye's voyageurs. In December, 1736, ice had forced him to winter at the mouth of Vermilion River, across Crane Lake. Two hundred and twenty-

25

one years ago, in front of the fireplace in their small log cabin at the foot of the gorge, he and his companion, Eustache, must have spent a lonely Christmas night. About seventy-five years later Dr. John McLoughlin, a famous Nor'Wester, perhaps at that same spot, spent another Christmas night. But rum and a violin undoubtedly made this one gayer for him and his voyageur companions.

With these thoughts, I fell asleep.

October 1, 1958
GRAND PORTAGE, MINNESOTA
AT THE NORTHEASTERN TIP OF MINNESOTA, ON LAKE SUPERIOR

Yoᴜ'ʀᴇ sure you didn't forget anything — matches, soap, maps?" Millie was supervising right down to the last minute, watching us get into the car and looking a little envious.

"Nope, nothing. And we'll be careful," Belva laughed as she anticipated Millie's usual admonition.

John drove Belva, Harvi, and me from Crane Lake to Grand Portage. The packs containing our shelter and sustenance were loaded into the trunk; the canoe rode securely on the car-top carriers. It was a glorious autumn day.

After leaving Duluth we followed the highway along the north shore of Lake Superior. Through the blue haze on the lake, silhouetted against the distant, deeper blue shore, a long ore carrier dragged a plume of smoke from its rear funnel as it slowly made its way down the lake. Gulls wheeled and glided overhead. Waves of green water pounded the jagged black rocks on shore and burst into silver spray.

We passed Two Harbors, Gooseberry Falls, Split Rock Lighthouse, and continued on. To the east a simple straight line separated sky from the lake, whose surface was broken by the wind into scintillating points of light. Landward a complex line followed the notched profile of the hills whose pine-greened undulations were splashed here and there with the flame of maple and the gold of birch and aspen.

Winding past sheltering coves and headlands of Brobdingnagian proportions, crossing rivers whose waters tumble and rush through rocky gorges in wild exhilaration, the road brought us to Grand Marais. Here the Gunflint Trail takes off northwesterly through the Superior National Forest to Gunflint Lake and Saganaga, on the Minnesota-Ontario boundary.

Just beyond a few small fishing shacks, surrounded by nets hung to dry, we passed a beach. Belva wanted to stop and join the people who were there searching for agates. "No," I said. "No rocks for you this trip!"

Turning off the highway, we wound five miles over a narrow dirt road down to a small bay on the shore of Lake Superior, and came to a few scattered old houses and the restoration of a fort.

Here it was at last — Grand Portage — that great stepping-off place to the wilderness! Here was no bustle and flurry as in former days, only calm and quiet, except for the soft, shrill *tzee* of cedar waxwings who, with their black masks and erect crests, looked like pert bandits as they plundered the red berries of the mountain ash.

We got out of the car, stretched, and looked about.

The small, shallow bay, surrounded by hills of diabase and carved out of slate, starts to the northeast at Hat Point (Pointe aux Chapeaux). It sweeps inward to the mouth of a creek and out again to Raspberry Point (Pointe aux Framboise). At the entrance to the bay sits small Mutton Island.

In the shadow of Mount Rose a reconstruction of the North West Company's famed fort with its picketed stockade, corner towers, and Great Hall stands near shore, just south of the creek. In front of the fort an L-shaped dock extends into the lake.

28

On the fort's northwest corner, at the postern gate, starts the nine-mile grand portage to the Pigeon River. This portage was necessary to avoid the brawling rapids, cascades, and high falls which make the last twenty miles of Pigeon River unnavigable before it pours into Lake Superior. Following the creek upstream, the trail, in a broad curve, passes through a preglacial valley and its dike, heads into high wooded hills, and then continues through the forest to Fort Charlotte, above the first cascade on the Pigeon River.

"Have a good time and be careful," John said, after we had finished unloading the car. "I've got to be home before it gets too late."

"See you in a week or so." Belva waved goodbye.

After he left, Harvi and I looked for a suitable campsite while Belva wandered along the shore.

We pitched the tent under a pine on the portage path near the fort, blew up our air mattresses, spread our sleeping bags, settled our packs in the tent, and then gathered wood for a fire.

When we had finished I glanced toward the shore. There I saw Belva, teetering like a sandpiper as she bent to pick up objects and stood up to examine them.

"Come on," I shouted. "We're going to climb Mount Rose to get a better view of the bay."

"I'll be right there," she answered, and then hurried back through the tall grass and across the creek. "Wait until you see what I've found."

In one outstretched hand, she held several pieces of white clay pipes, used long ago by the voyageurs — two broken bowls, one with "W.G." stamped into the clay, the other with "T.D.," and four sections of stem worn smooth by the sand and water. In the other hand she had an Indian scraper and spearpoint. No small find for a half hour's search, these meager tokens told of activity here in days past.

We struggled up the steep trail leading to the top of Mount Rose — Belva, Harvi, and I. Arriving at the top, red-faced and puffing, we saw the setting sun tint the sky a deep rose, while the sprawling lake reflected an opalescent burgundy.

As I sat on a boulder and looked out over Lake Superior, I wondered what lure the setting sun had held for men of adventure in ages past. What

29

irresistible urges had driven them to this very spot and on through the Quetico-Superior waterways westward, ever following the sun?

Of course I had read in learned accounts that, in the fifteenth and sixteenth centuries, the burning desire for the riches of the Orient, as well as an innate urge to follow the sun, had led explorers, filled with the energy of the Renaissance, across the Atlantic. But instead of reaching the shores of China and India, they found a new land. Thinking this continent was only an insignificant barrier to their goal, they began probing its bays and inlets, soon realizing these new lands were not just on the perimeter of Asia. As they looked for a waterway through the land mass, they became aware that only two existed — one through Hudson's Bay, the other through the St. Lawrence–Lake Superior waterways.

By mid-seventeenth century the English and French had done well. Hudson, under the Cross of St. George, had broken through the ice into Hudson's Bay; Champlain, under the fleur de lis, had pushed up the St. Lawrence, following Cartier, and then with the aid of Brûlé and Nicolet, discovered the Great Lakes.

Now a false geographical premise — the existence of a Northwest Passage — and the hairy coat of a brown rodent with a flat, broad tail and yellow, chisel teeth — the fur of the beaver — would draw adventurers through these two approaches to the heart of the continent and beyond. It was the sons of New France on the St. Lawrence who led the way, over the Quetico-Superior canoe route and on through the water trails of the north.

Step by step these dashing Frenchmen began to penetrate farther into the *pays d'en haut*. Along the way they halted frequently to consider the use of waterways other than those of the Quetico-Superior. For example, they actively considered the more advantageous Hudson's Bay approach. In the intermittent battles that ensued — a period of capture and recapture, of blazing forts and sinking ships — the French almost succeeded in ousting the English from the bay. They even considered the Missouri route, later used by Lewis and Clark. But their efforts were always frustrated, now by power struggles between courts in faraway Europe, again by lack of royal finance, hostility from the Indians, or struggles with rivals in the New World.

30

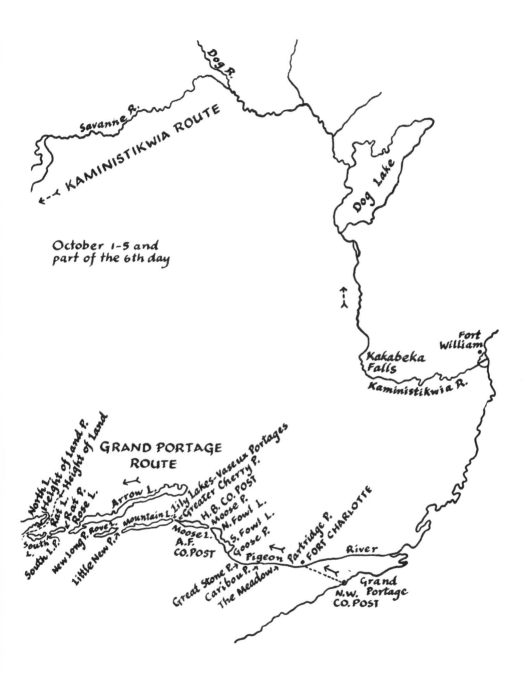

Dog R.

Savanne R.

←↗ KAMINISTIKWIA ROUTE

Dog Lake

October 1-5 and
part of the 6th day

↑
↖

Fort
William

Kakabeka
Falls

Kaministikwia R.

GRAND PORTAGE
ROUTE

North L.
Height of Land P.
Rat L. Height of Land
Rose L.
South L. P.
South L.
New Long P.
Rove L.
Little New P. ↗
Mountain L.
Arrow L. →
Lily Lakes-Vaseux Portages
Greater Cherry P.
H.B. CO. POST
Moose P.
N. Fowl L.
S. Fowl L.
Goose P.
Moose L.
A.F. CO. POST
Great Stone R. →
Caribou P. ↗
The Meadow →
Pigeon
Partridge P. →
FORT CHARLOTTE
River
←
↖
Grand Portage
N.W. CO. POST

As they searched for a Northwest Passage, new trade areas for beaver were opened. The wealth in peltries obtained in these areas, in turn, helped to finance their further explorations. And often, as they competed for furs with the Hudson's Bay Company in the north and with the New England colonists in the south, the hunt for the Western Sea was extended. At the same time both activities helped them to maintain their hold on the New World.

"What on earth are you dreaming about?" Belva's voice broke into my thoughts about the progress of the French towards Grand Portage.

I answered, "Setting suns, Frenchmen, and waterways," but my words were unattended. She had disappeared behind some trees, intruding herself into the private life of a chickadee family. Close by, Harvi napped on a bed of moss, his legs crossed and his head resting on clasped hands.

Since Belva and Harvi were so busily occupied, I looked up at Hat Point. A feeling of awe crept over me as I thought of the succession of figures who had, through the years, paddled around it into the bay on their way to the Northwest. I wondered who had been first, then thought of those that followed.

Perhaps the first were the *coureurs de bois*. They left no records, but Washington Irving described them for us. "These men would set out from Montreal with canoes well stocked with goods, with arms and ammunition, and would make their way up the mazy and wandering rivers that interlace the vast forests of the Canadas, coasting the most remote lakes, and creating new wants and habitudes among the natives. Sometimes they sojourned for months among them, assimilating to their tastes and habits with the happy facility of Frenchmen, adopting in some degree the Indian dress, and not infrequently taking to themselves Indian wives.

"Twelve, fifteen, eighteen months would often elapse without any tidings of them, when they would come sweeping their way down the Ottawa in full glee, their canoes laden down with the packs of beaver skins. . . .

"Many of these *coureurs des bois* became so accustomed to the Indian mode of living, and the perfect freedom of the wilderness, that they lost all relish for civilization, and identified themselves with the savages among whom they dwelt, or could only be distinguished from them by superior licentiousness."

32

Or perhaps the first were the Jesuit priests, who were establishing missions among the Indians on Lake Superior.

Maybe Pierre d'Esprit Radisson and his brother-in-law, Médard Chouart, sieur des Groseilliers, led the way. But then, who could tell? Radisson wrote about his second voyage years after it occurred, only to impress the courts of Europe, not to give an accurate account of his travels. On this voyage he and Groseilliers slipped away one night in 1659 from Three Rivers on the St. Lawrence and slowly made their way to the shores of Lake Superior. During this voyage, we know, without being able to follow their complete route, that they learned of the tremendous abundance of furs in the north country. At the same time they became acquainted with the two approaches to this wealth. And they also became aware of the advantages of the route through Hudson's Bay over the one through the St. Lawrence. Their knowledge became embodied in the Hudson's Bay Company.

Certainly the first man to record that he had been here and beyond was Pierre Gaultier de Varennes, sieur de La Vérendrye. Accompanied by three of his four sons, Jean Baptiste, Pierre, and François; his nephew, La Jemeraye; Father Mesaiger, the missionary attached to the expedition; and fifty voyageurs, he arrived here on August 26, 1731.

Before using the route, La Vérendrye had carefully laid his plans to search for the Western Sea. First he joined the family fur business, after returning to his birthplace at Three Rivers with the scars of nine wounds suffered in the king's service in France. Later, at the age of forty-three, he applied to the governor for the post at Lake Nipigon, and got it. While at this post he acquainted himself "with the route through different savages, who all made the same statement, that there are three routes or rivers which lead to the great river of the West." So he "had a map made of these three rivers, in order that I might be able to choose the shortest and easiest road." An Indian attached to the post named Auchagah drew him a map on birchbark, our first of the border lakes, "showing the three rivers which flow into Lake Superior, namely the one called Fond du Lac River [St. Louis], the Nantouagan [Pigeon], and the Kaministikwia." He continued, "The two latter are those on which everything is marked with exactness . . . lakes, rapids, portages, the side on which the portage must be made, and the heights of land . . . Comparing these two routes, the river Nantouagan [Pigeon] . . . is, it seems to me, the one to be preferred. It has, it is true, forty-two portages, while the Kaministikwia has only twenty-two; but, on the other hand, it has no rapids, while the other has twelve, two of which are long and very shallow. Besides, the road is straight and one third shorter."

Over the years dauntless La Vérendrye and his sons passed many times through Grand Portage and the Quetico-Superior waterways in their search for the Sea of the West. He built posts at Rainy Lake (Fort St. Pierre), Lake of the Woods (Fort St. Charles, his headquarters), and Lake Winnipeg (Fort Maurepas), as well as lesser ones. These posts were strategically located to carry on discovery and to intercept the flow of Indian trade to Hudson's Bay. From them he eventually reached the Black Hills and the Saskatchewan River, although he had failed in his attempt to find the elusive passage. These discoveries were to be financed by his trade with the Indians; but he was allowed no profit from the wealth gained in this trade, not even his expenses. La Vérendrye finally resigned, in bad health, after withstanding eleven years of fraud, debt, censure, and disappointment.

In 1740 while La Vérendrye was still using the route, an illiterate French half-breed, Joseph la France, passed through on his way to Hudson's Bay. His trip was the first to connect the Lake Superior and Hudson's Bay approaches to the fur country.

Many French fur traders, would-be explorers, followed after La Vérendrye's resignation, including his successors — de Noyelles, St. Pierre, and La Corne. They only further exploited the fur trade, until France lost Canada to Britain in 1763.

Soon after the conquest of Canada, Thomas Curry, Joseph and Thomas Frobisher, Peter Pond, Alexander Henry the elder, and other English, Scotch, and Yankee traders came from Montreal, seeking their fortune in furs in the Northwest.

Finally, the great company of Nor'Westers came to use Grand Portage as their inland depot and rendezvous, and to build a fur empire throughout the North. From 1780 — during the American Revolution when the country west of the Alleghenies was little known, to 1804 — when they abandoned Grand Portage — they rounded Hat Point in their loaded canoes.

My reverie was broken as Harvi awoke, uncrossed his legs, stretched, and moved over beside me. "Harvi, what do you imagine it looked like down there when the voyageurs and fur traders were here?" I nodded toward the fort.

"Like it does now, I guess," he answered.

"Maybe this will give you an idea," I said, as I looked through my notes and pulled out Macdonell's account of Grand Portage. Perhaps the best description of Grand Portage, it was written when Macdonell went through as a clerk of the North West Company on his first trip west in July, 1793.

As I started to read, Belva returned and sat down on the rock beside me. "Leaving *pointe au pére* we paddled two pipes and put to shore to give the men time to clean themselves, while we breakfasted — this done a short pipe brought us to *Pointe au Chapeaux* around which we got a sight of the long wished for Grand Portage. The beach was covered with spectators to see us arrive, our canoe went well and the crew sung paddling songs in a vociferous manner.

"The Grand Portage is situated in the bottom of a shallow Bay perhaps three miles deep and about one league and a half wide at its mouth from *Pointe aux Chapeaux* to *pointe a la Framboise* having a small Island just opposite the fort about half way from one of these points to the other: on a low spot which rises gently from the Lake. The pickets are not above fifteen to twenty paces from the waters edge. Immediately back of the Fort is a lofty round Sugar Loaf mountain the base of which comes close to the Picket on the North West Side."

"Harvi, we're sitting on Sugar Loaf mountain, you know," broke in Belva.

I continued, "The Gates are shut alyways [*sic*] after sunset and the Bourgeois and clerks Lodge in houses within the pallisades, where there are two Sentries keeping a look out all night cheifly for fear of accident by fire. A clerk a guide and four men are considered watch enough. These are Montreal engagees.

"The North men while here live in tents of different sizes pitched at random, the people of each post having a camp by themselves and through their camp passes the road of the portage. They are separated from the Montrealeans by a brook. The Portage is three leagues from one navigation to the other which caused great expense and trouble to the company. The men have Six Livers [*livres*] . . . for every peice of Goods or pack of Furs they carry from one end of it to the other . . .

"All the buildings within the Fort are sixteen in number made with cedar and white spruce fir split with whip saws after being suquared [*sic*], the Roofs are couvered with shingles of Cedar and Pine, most of their posts, Doors, and windows, are painted with spanish brown. Six of these buildings are Store Houses for the company's Merchandize and Furs &c. The rest are dwelling houses shops compting house and Mess House — they have also a wharf or kay for their vessel to unload and Load at. . . . Between two and three hundred yards to the East of the N.W. Fort beyond the Pork eaters camp is the spot Mess[rs] David and Peter Grant [leaders of an opposition group to the N.W. Co.] have selected to build upon, as yet they have done nothing to it but marking out the four corners of the ground they mean to occupy with posts stuck in the ground. . . . A full allowance to a voyageur while at this Poste is a Quart of Lyed Indian Corn or maize, and one ounce of Greece."

"Hmm," Harvi murmured as I finished.

"Macdonell's description is my favorite," added Belva.

As we sat looking down at the reconstructed fort, I visualized a day here — say in early July, 1802 — and described it to Harvi.

At that time Grand Portage teemed with activity. It was the annual meeting place for the two agents and their voyageurs from Montreal, and for the wintering partners, clerks, and northmen from the *pays d'en haut.* To Grand Portage the Nor'Westers came to determine policy, to assign trading departments, to apportion profits, and to revel.

It was the center of the fur empire of the North West Company as it ruled the vast territory extending to the Arctic tundra and to the Pacific slopes. Through this point funneled the furs gathered the preceding winter, to be counted, bundled, and stamped, before proceeding on their way to Montreal and the great fur marts of Europe and Asia. The riches gained from the furs played no small part in the power struggles in Europe and in the unfolding destinies of Canada and the United States. Through Grand

36

Portage from Montreal, came the trade goods ordered in England — blankets and other woolen goods, arms and ammunition, twist and carrot tobacco, ironmongery and cutlery, copper and brass kettles, beads and trinkets, and thousands of gallons of high wines from Canada. These goods were packed in ninety-pound *pièces* to be distributed to the wintering posts scattered at immense distances among the lakes and streams of the wilderness.

The camp of the northmen, cut through by the portage trail, stood behind the fort. It consisted of different-sized, weathered tents belonging to some seven hundred *hommes du nord*. Those voyageurs left their wintering posts in canoes loaded with furs, bound for Grand Portage every spring as soon as the ice was out.

Justifiably boasting, "Je suis un homme du nord" (I am a man of the north), they led Spartan lives through the long, bleak winters on a diet, when it was available, of fish, game, wild rice, and pemmican. Braving the bitterly cold winds, they went through the forests on snowshoes, or over frozen lakes with dog teams to trade with the Indians, to communicate with other posts, and to get food.

Now, at Grand Portage, they had two full weeks of gambling, feasting, drinking, and wenching, before they returned to their posts with trade goods. With feathers cocked in their red woolen caps and the fringes of their bright-patterned sashes aswing, they went swaggering about the camp, some at an uncertain gait, bragging of their ability "to carry, paddle, walk, and sing with any man" and of their prowess with dog teams, dusky maidens, and drink. Gathered in groups, smoking their clay pipes and gesticulating, they were, I am sure, telling many a bawdy story and tall tale of their winter experiences which, with each telling, grew taller.

The swashbucklers of the fur trade, they frequently would steal across the creek into the camp of the novice pork-eaters to ridicule and so start a fight, occasionally winding up in the jail, the *pot au beurre*, maintained at the fort for uncontrollable voyageurs.

The camp of the pork-eaters, or *mangeurs du lard*, so called from their eating lyed corn and grease, was composed of rows of upturned canoes, which served as their shelter while here. Separated from the northmen by the creek to prevent battles, it was east of the stockade. In their camp, consisting of some four hundred men, many comers and goers, as the pork-eaters were also called, were gathered about their canoes, waterproofing the seams of the bark by applying pine gum melted with a torch.

This group of voyageurs brought the trade goods from Lachine, eight miles below Montreal, to Grand Portage in Montreal canoes. These *canots du maître* were so large — thirty-five to forty feet and weighing five hundred pounds — that they carried sixty-five *pièces*, weighing ninety pounds each, six hundred pounds of biscuit, two hundred pounds of pork, three bushels of peas, a crew of ten men and their baggage, and had to be portaged bottom up by four men at the ends and two in the middle.

As soon as the ice was out in early May the voyageurs proceeded to Ste. Anne's Church at Lachine to perform a religious custom which Peter Pond described thus: "Heare is a small Box with a Hole in the top for ye Reseption of a Little Money for the Hole [Holy] father or to say a small Mass for those who Put a small Sum in the Box. Scars a Voiger but stops hear and Puts in his mite and By that Meanes thay Suppose thay are Protected."

Then with forests and lakes, portage trails, silence, singing, and kegs of wine ahead, eighteen hundred miles from Grand Portage, they swung their canoes up the famous Ottawa River route to Lake Nipissing and from there down the French River to Georgian Bay on Lake Huron and to Sault Ste. Marie. From the Sault, they skirted the northern shore of Lake Superior and proceeded to Grand Portage.

The Indian village, a collection of huts or wigiwams covered with sheets of birchbark, lay along the shore of Grand Portage bay. At times several thousand Chippewas gathered here. The children were running about and playing, the dogs barking and yelping at their heels. The women were busy with their many chores. Some of the men sat around talking and smoking, others were gathered around stake enclosures working on the birch canoes in various stages of completion inside them. Some of these enclosures contained only light tough frames of cedar. In others the cedar frames were covered with pieces of bark sewn together with wattap — cedar or spruce roots. Still others held completed canoes that were painted with a decorative touch — the gunwales green, red, and white and the prows with Indian heads, pipes, or some other familiar object. Seventy canoes came out of this primitive factory yearly for use in the trade.

38

Over the portage from Fort Charlotte groups of northmen were arriving. For here, Sir Alexander Mackenzie, one of the North West Company's great explorers, wrote, they "are regaled with bread, pork, butter, liquor, and tobacco, and such as have not entered into agreements during the winter, which is customary, are contracted with, to return and perform the voyage for one, two, or three years: their accounts are also settled, and such as choose to send any of their earnings to Canada, receive drafts to transmit to their relations or friends . . ." Time was short for renewing acquaintances, news from home, and revelry; for "as soon as they can be got ready, which requires no more than a fortnight, they are again dispatched to their respective departments."

Trotting across the portage, in the other direction, were a few late pork-eaters with two, three, or more packs of trade goods on their backs. At Fort Charlotte they would exchange the goods for packs of furs, which they would then carry back over the portage. One group of select pork-eaters had taken trade goods to the Athabaska House at the Rainy Lake (Lac la Pluie) post. The far-famed Athabaskan voyageurs, haughty with self-endowed superiority, were the only absentees from Grand Portage. Coming from two thousand miles away, they could not make the rendezvous. Because of the short summer, the rivers and lakes would be choked with ice before their return, so they came down only as far as Rainy Lake with their furs, where a special house was built for them.

Out in the bay, rounding Hat Point, a brigade of canoes was approaching at top speed, the voyageurs singing their heads off and furiously dipping their paddles in the cold, clear water to reach Grand Portage. They had stopped before rounding Hat Point, near Pointe aux Père Jesuite, to wash, comb, and perhaps braid their long black hair, and to deck themselves out in their best sashes, shirts, and red caps. When their canoes pulled up to the dock in front of the fort, a burst of musket fire cracked across the bay; voyageurs, clerks, and Indians hurried to greet them.

In deeper water, in the lee of Mutton Island, a sailing vessel of fifty to seventy tons burden lay at anchor, unable to come closer with full cargo. It had just completed its run from Sault Ste. Marie to Grand Portage. Voyageurs were busy emptying its hold of flour and corn from Detroit, and maple sugar, tallow, and gum from Michilimackinac.

Below me the men of the XY Company were "busy building a very fine 'fort' upon the hill," for they only "had a few buildings, a few hundred yards to the East of the N.W. C°." (Nelson). The XY Company was formed when a third of the Nor'Westers broke away from the parent organization in dissatisfaction. Under the leadership of Sir Alexander Mackenzie, after his retirement from the North West Company, they maintained competitive posts throughout the fur country. These Potties (a corruption of *les petits* disparagingly used by the Nor'Westers) continued opposition until 1804, then reunited with the North West Company.

While all this activity was going on outside the fort, inside the two agents from Montreal and the wintering partners were busy with other problems. During the year, before their meeting in council, each had important functions to perform in the conduct of the trade. The agents were charged with purchasing, packing, and forwarding trade goods, provisions, and liquor, as well as hiring workers, acting as attorneys for the partners, and marketing the furs. The partners had charge of the various trading departments in the interior, and actively engaged in trading during the winter.

Here the agents and partners were meeting to carry out their common business. They heard the annual financial report submitted by the agents. They discussed trade practices to be followed during the ensuing year: changes in trading areas, location of employees, apportionment of goods, promotions, retirements, and new rules for the conduct of trade. To decide each issue a majority of fifty-two votes was required, each one present having only one vote.

As the agents and partners — the *bourgeois* — were conducting their business, the clerks worked in the "compting house" and the other storehouses within the fort. Apprenticed to the trade for five to seven years with opportunity for advancement to partnership, the clerks were in charge of posts during the long winters, keeping journals and supervising the trade in their areas. Now they were settling accounts and signing new agreements with employees, receiving and packing furs into bundles, and making trade goods up into *pièces*.

Washington Irving, who had talked and visited with many of the partners and agents in Montreal, vividly described the annual conference where "the aristocratical character of the Briton shone forth magnificently, or rather the feudal spirit of the Highlander."

Each partner "repaired there as to a meeting of parliament," feeling "like the chieftain of a Highland clan." But the agents from Montreal "were the lords of the ascendant; coming from the midst of luxurious and ostentatious life, they quite eclipsed their compeers from the woods, whose forms and faces had been battered and hardened by hard living and hard service, and whose garments and equipments were all the worse for wear."

The meetings "were held in great state, for every member felt as if sitting in parliament, and every retainer and dependent looked up to the assemblage with awe, as to the house of lords. There was a vast deal of solemn deliberation, and hard Scottish reasoning, with an occasional swell of pompous declamation."

But "these grave and weighty councils were alternated by huge feasts and revels, like some of the old feasts described in Highland castles. The tables in the great banqueting room groaned under the weight of game of all kinds; of venison from the woods, and fish from the lakes, with hunter's delicacies, such as buffaloes' tongues and beavers' tails; and various luxuries from Montreal, all served up by experienced cooks brought for the purpose. There was no stint of generous wine, for it was a hard-drinking period, a time of loyal toasts, and bacchanalian songs, and brimming bumpers.

"While the chiefs thus reveled in hall, and made the rafters resound with bursts of loyalty and old Scottish songs, chanted in voices cracked and sharpened by the northern blast, their merriment was echoed and prolonged by a mongrel legion of retainers, Canadian voyageurs, half breeds, Indian hunters, and vagabond hangers on, who feasted sumptuously without on the crumbs that fell from their table, and made the welkin ring with old French ditties, mingled with Indian yelps and yellings."

Then, by the first of August, the annual meeting was over, the silence of the forest fell again.

Today, "its council chamber is silent and deserted; its banquet-hall no longer echoes to the burst of loyalty, or the 'auld world' ditty; the lords of the lakes and forests have passed away."

"Let's go down and see what's in the Great Hall where the lords deliberated, feasted, and reveled," said Belva, getting up to go, after I had finished telling Harvi what went on here years ago.

In the Great Hall, "The proprietors, clerks, guides, and interpreters mess together, to the number of sometimes an hundred, at several tables, in one large hall, the provision consisting of bread, salt pork, beef, hams, fish, and venison, butter, peas, Indian corn, potatoes, tea, spirits, wine, &c. and plenty of milk, for which purpose several milch cows are constantly kept," explained Mackenzie. We admired the north canoe hanging from the ceiling and the numerous displays of Chippewa handicraft. Hung on the walls were placards briefly explaining the history of Grand Portage under three flags — the fleur de lis, the Grand Union flag, and the Stars and Stripes.

One explained that in 1778 five hundred persons were here, the interior trade amounting to £40,000 annually, that these traders "have a general Rendezvous at the Portage, and for the refreshing and comforting those who are employed in the more distant voyages the Traders from hence have built tolerable Houses; and in order to cover them from any insult from the numerous savage Tribes, who resort there during that time, have made stockades around them." No wonder Alexander Henry the elder remarked, in 1775, that he "found the traders in a state of extreme reciprocal hostility, each pursuing his interests in such a manner as might most injure his neighbour."

The placard went on to say that, although the French had probably maintained a post previously, the first fort was built here in 1778. In that year animosity generated among the independent Canadian traders in their bitter competition for the Indians' furs, the dangers of Indian attack, and the possibility that the traders might seek greater profits by illegally selling their British goods to colonial troops whose duty in the Revolution found them in Illinois country led John Askin, commissary at Mackinac, to send Lieutenant Thomas Bennett of the Eighth Regiment of Foot and twelve soldiers to build the fort at the expense of the traders. This fort was probably the nucleus around which the North West Company built its great post two years later.

Another placard explained that when the Bureau of Indian Affairs decided to reconstruct the fort, a series of exploratory trenches were dug,

42

revealing the location of the stockade and buildings; reconstruction began in 1938. Still another recounted the dedication of Grand Portage and the reconstructed fort as a national historic site on August 9, 1951.

On a table was a copy of a notarized engagement which the voyageurs, as *engagées*, were required to sign before entering the service of the North West Company— *lequel s'est volontairement Engagé et s'Engagé par ces Présents à Messrs*. M'Tavish, Frobisher, E C°. The voyageurs came to Montreal to sign these engagements with their usual X's. These men, the Pierres, the Amables, and the Jean Baptistes, thereby agreed to serve one to three years, and not to desert nor to aid rival traders. In return the company promised to pay every year twelve hundred livres, two blankets, two shirts, two pairs of trousers, and fourteen pounds of carrot tobacco to foremen and steersmen, and to the milieux eight hundred livres, the same equipment, and ten pounds of tobacco.

We stumbled through the French on an 1802 bill of lading for a Montreal canoe— Canot 25: *Ballots de Tabac* (packages of tobacco), *de Jambons* (hams), *Barils de High Wines*, which I was sure the voyageurs handled with special care on the portages!, *de Lard, de Poudre* (gunpowder), *de Boeuf, Caisses de Fer* (crates of ironmongery), *de Chapeaux, de Couteaux* (knives), *de Fusils* (guns), *de Pièges* (traps), *Sacs de Balles* (sacks of bullets)— on and on it went to a total of 84 *pièces*. Then followed *Les noms des hommes* (the names of the voyageurs assigned to the canoe), *les Vivres* (the food supply), and finally *Les Agrès* (the equipment for the canoe), which included two oilcloths to cover the goods, a sail, a sponge for bailing out the canoe, an axe, a frying pan, a kettle, a bench line for towing, a roll of birchbark for repairs, a bundle of wattap to sew the seams in the birchbark, and gum for waterproofing the seams.

Then we returned to camp. Our tent stood where those of the northmen had been, for we meant to become northmen too.

Later that evening, we watched a radiance spread in ripples over the lake as, from its eastern rim, a gilt, pumpkin moon slowly emerged. Rising higher, its warm light revealed the dim outline of the bay, the stockade, and Mount Rose. The soft, sibilant swish of the waves washing over the pebbly shore whispered to us through the hushed air of autumn as we sat relaxed around our campfire.

43

Harvi gazed at the stockade. "You know, Harvi, the big event here every year was the ball," I said.

"Why don't you read Harmon's *Journals* for him?" Belva asked.

Daniel Harmon became a North West Company clerk in 1800. Thereafter, the deeply religious Vermont Yankee spent nineteen years of his life in the service of the company, eight of them beyond the Rocky Mountains as superintendent of all its affairs.

Harvi stirred the fire. Sparks shot upward toward the stars. With firelight flickering over my notes, I read, "In the evening, the gentlemen of the place dressed, and we had a famous ball, in the dining room. For musick, we had the bag-pipe, the violin and the flute, which added much to the interest of the occasion. At the ball, there was a number of the ladies of this country; and I was surprised to find that they could conduct with so much propriety, and dance so well."

Everyone went to the ball dressed in all his finery. In gray coats, breeches, and colorful silk vests, the agents, partners, and clerks came from their log houses in the stockade; the pork-eaters with clean colored shirts and sashes from their rows of upturned canoes; the northmen in plumed red caps, buckskin shirts, breechcloths, leggings, and sashes kept for such special occasions from their camp of tents. The Indians came too —chiefs in red and blue coats with medals around their necks and swords at their sides, maidens in doeskin with beaded floral designs, braves in buckskin and with gaudily painted faces, and squaws with papooses.

Gathering in the Great Hall, which was ablaze with many candles, they soon broke into Highland flings, reels, and square dances to the accompanying din of skirling pipes, squeaking fiddles, and screeching flutes. The dances grew gayer as the level of high wine in the kegs became lower. Frequently a lithe figure in a doeskin dress, followed by the brawny form of a bright-sashed voyageur, would slip quietly through a door into the concealing darkness of the warm July night. As appetites grew sharper a table was spread with platters of trout, whitefish, buffalo tongue, venison, and butter. At dawn the party broke up, to be discussed many times during the long winter ahead.

Tonight, behind the stockade, the Great Hall was dark and quiet. I sat staring into the leaping flames of our fire, gripped by two emotions.

44

One was intense anticipation of the morning and the start of the trip —
and perhaps some trepidation too. After all, didn't La Vérendrye's men
mutiny when they arrived here? The explorer wrote "all our people, in
dismay at the length of the portage, three leagues, mutinied and loudly
demanded that I should turn back." I reminded myself that La Vérendrye's competitors back home had bribed the men to turn back, but my
misgivings returned as I thought of St. Pierre, who also protested when
he arrived here in 1750: "This is the first of the western posts [Grand
Portage] . . . Bad as I had imagined the roads, I was surprised at the
reality. There are thirty-eight carrying places; the first of these is four
leagues, and the least of all the others is a quarter of a league. The remainder of the road was not more attractive; on the contrary, I was assured it
was infinitely worse, besides being dangerous. In fact, I had time to feel
that there was the constant risk of not only losing goods and provisions,
but even life itself."

The other emotion was deeper, indefinable, inexpressible. Perhaps it
could be called reverence for the past. It was the feeling one has in places
where events of great historical significance have occurred. I felt the living presence of Alexander Henry the elder, Peter Pond, Sir Alexander
Mackenzie, and David Thompson. They had paused here many times, and
then continued on their way to unexplored, unconquered lands beyond. I
thought of the accomplishments of these Nor'Westers in those lands —
achievements important in the evolving drama of our continent.

Alexander Henry the elder, a Yankee, was one of the first of the new
traders to enter the *pays d'en haut* after the conquest of Canada. On his
way to the interior he narrowly escaped death at Michilimackinac during
Pontiac's Indian uprising in 1763. Only the mercy of an Indian woman,
who hid him in an attic, kept him alive while all the other white men were
massacred in the yard below. After this, he traded in the Lake Superior
area before going, in 1775, to the Saskatchewan River country. During
the next few years he became familiar with this river system, and was the
first to point out its importance to the fur trade. At forty-two he retired to
become a general merchant in Montreal. Later he sold his interests in the
Indian country to the North West Company.

About the time Alexander Henry the elder went to the Saskatchewan, another shrewd Yankee, Peter Pond, entered the fur country. After serving for several years in the French and Indian wars, he became interested in the fur trade, and spent the next ten years in the region of the Upper Mississippi. In 1775 he went to the Northwest and nine years later, at forty-three, became one of the first members of the North West Company. In the interior his violent temper, sensitivity, and egotism frequently got him in trouble. Among other things he was accused of the murder of two traders. He was later cleared, but the accusation proved to be the last in the long series of difficulties which finally led to his retirement. Nevertheless, his achievements were of the greatest importance. He was the first to cross the famous Methye portage, and so opened the beaver-rich Athabaska country to the North West Company. This wealth became the life-blood of the Nor'Westers and finally precipitated its struggle with the Hudson's Bay Company. He instituted the use of pemmican to supply the long lines of communication to the trade areas. Despite his meager training, he drew the first map of the Northwest, thus laying the foundation for its further exploration.

Alexander Mackenzie, perhaps the greatest of all the Nor'Westers, became, after eight years in the fur trade, a partner in the North West Company in 1787. The next year he was put in charge of Fort Chipewyan on Lake Athabaska, where Pond taught him all he had learned about the Northwest. A year later, in 1789, the handsome, intrepid Scotch explorer made his famous journey down the river which now bears his name to the Arctic in search of a Northwest Passage. In 1793 he was the first white man traveling overland in northern latitudes to reach the Pacific Ocean. After six more years, dissatisfied with the North West Company for not recognizing his achievements, he went to England, where he published his *Voyages* and was knighted. Returning to Canada, Sir Alexander headed the XY Company for two years until it reunited with the North West Company in 1804. He was an inactive Nor'Wester for sixteen years more, until his death.

David Thompson, the greatest land geographer of all time, came to know the border lakes well. During the twenty-eight years that he was in the fur trade, this courageous and honorable man explored and mapped almost the entire Northwest with only "a Sextant of ten inches radius,

46

with Quicksilver and parallel glasses, an excellent Achromatic Telescope; a lesser for common use; drawing instruments, and two thermometers; all made by Dolland." So accurate were his maps that one could almost superimpose them on the aerial maps of today.

Born in England in 1770, he was sent after his father's death to a charitable institution, the Grey Coat School at Westminster. There he showed marked aptitude in geography and mathematics. At the age of fourteen he was apprenticed to the Hudson's Bay Company, having met the company's qualifications in its request to the school for boys with navigational knowledge. During his fourteen years' service with the Hudson's Bay Company he spent most of his time trading on the bay, but he also traveled some four thousand miles of waterways in the interior, surveying over three thousand of them.

Disgruntled with the Hudson's Bay Company for not allowing him to explore further, he joined the ranks of the Nor'Westers and so, in 1797, traveling from Reindeer Lake to Grand Portage, he passed over the border waters to become a clerk in the North West Company.

In August of the same year he left Grand Portage on the first of his long and arduous expeditions to explore and map the vast empire of the North West Company. He went west to the Red River and the Mandan posts on the Missouri River, and returned east to the headwaters of the Mississippi. He went on to Fond du Lac, the south shore of Lake Superior, and the Sault, making notes and observations of latitude and longitude as he went.

Becoming a partner in 1804, he continued to map the Northwest, and explored the Columbia River for the first time. On retirement in 1812, he prepared a huge map, fifteen miles to the inch, based on his observations throughout the Northwest. Upon completion, this map, which later became the basis of all such maps, was hung in the Great Hall at Fort William for all the Nor'Westers to use and admire.

"Are you going to sit there all night?" Belva asked from the tent.

The coals of the fire were rimmed white with ashes. A thin wisp of gray smoke floated lazily skyward.

Harvi yawned. "It's going to be a long, tough day tomorrow. I'm turning in too."

We crawled into the tent and soon fell asleep.

October 2. ON THE GRAND PORTAGE TRAIL
FROM LAKE SUPERIOR TO FORT CHARLOTTE ON THE PIGEON RIVER

Up from the lake rose the sun, pushing crimson streaks into the sky, to promise a flawless autumn day for the start of our trip. We hurried about excitedly, gulping breakfast, breaking camp, and making ready our packs.

"We're off!" I shouted.

"Definitely," Belva answered, as she shrugged herself into her pack.

Harvi only smiled and shifted the canoe.

At 7 A.M., Harvi with the canoe perched on his shoulders and Belva and I loaded with packs started over the nine-mile portage to Pigeon River, the first of many such trails in Minnesota used by white men. We had begun our trip over the first two hundred miles of the explorers' and fur traders' route from Grand Portage to the Northwest. On our way through the boundary waters we would paddle through the same lakes, carry over the same portages, and camp on the same shores as they had.

Having used this trail for centuries, the Indians pointed it out to the first white men to come here. One of many ancient trails traveled by early man for hunting, exploration, and trade, it takes its place in history along with the great trade routes of the world.

The *grande portage* follows the creek a short distance, crosses it, and then continues on in a rise of five hundred feet to Fort Charlotte. As we started over it our fear of not finding the way was soon dispelled. The path, deep in leaves of gold, was easy to follow. It had been packed hard by thousands of moccasined feet tramping over it in ages past. Only a few small aspen and birch pushed up here and there through its compact soil.

Though the trail did not appear to rise abruptly, after half a mile my legs ached, my breathing was deep and hard, my vision was blurred with sweat. I crumpled down to rest. What a voyageur I would make!

For them it was easy. The voyageurs, Mackenzie noted on this portage, were "so inured . . . to this kind of labour, . . . some of them set off with two packages of ninety pounds each, and return with two others of the same weight, in the course of six hours, being a distance of eighteen miles over hills and mountains." Their engagements stated they had "to carry eight packages of such goods and provisions as are necessary for the interior country" and "if more goods are necessary to be transported, they are allowed a Spanish dollar for each package."

And this was only my first *posé*! Fifteen more to go. A *posé* to the voyageurs was a place to deposit their packs on the portages. They carried all the cargo to one *posé* before going any further. This maneuver afforded better protection from marauders than if the goods had been left scattered along the trail. A *posé* occurred every third to half of a mile, and so the number indicated the length of a portage.

As I sat resting I wondered if it had been easier for the voyageurs because of their different method of carrying packs. Certainly our method, with its high back carry from shoulder straps, chokes off breathing and uses muscles not adapted to strains. I remembered Delafield's description of their method as he crossed the portage. "The mode of carrying is by a portage collar, so called, which is a long leather strap with a broad band in the center to place on the forehead. The load is tied by the ends of it, the band placed on the forehead, & by stooping the man throws the one

49

piece tied into the hollow of his back, his hands then being at liberty, he throws another piece on top of it which fills up the load to the back of his head, bending forward, he takes it over his post [*posé*] on a slow trot, a very fast walk with bended knees. The two pieces are carried with more ease than one, on account of the direction of the weight upon the body. . . . A man will, when he pleases however, carry three pieces, but it is not required of them. The Canadians [voyageurs] surpass all others upon the portage. My American of the party was very awkward at first, but soon carried light loads with ease, and it soon proved that in no other manner, so great a weight could be carried on the portage as by the collar."

A mile up the trail we came to the site of the "1688 rock," and stopped to rest. Now on display in the Great Hall, the rock was found here several years ago covered with grass and moss. Carved on it is the date *1688*, below which is the name *George*, and slightly below this the name *Na ga nib*. While its authenticity remains to be proved, experts say the date might mark the one-year period of neutrality, agreed on in 1687 by France and England, during which each country could establish prior claims to territory in the Northwest.

Soon we were on our way again through the crisp October morning. Now, in the fall, heat, flies, and mosquitoes did not bedevil us as they had the voyageurs who, in mid-July, trotted the hot and still trail half-naked. They must have sweated and panted, and swatted many a mosquito and fly on their bare thighs and buttocks, muttering at the same time, "à misère," or even "sacajé chien." Mud did not bother us either, but it certainly did the voyageurs. Alexander Henry the younger wrote in 1800, "The portage was very bad in some places, being knee deep in mud and clay, and so slippery as to make walking tedious."

At noon, after following the trail across the highway, we stopped for lunch, with squirrels chattering and scolding from all directions. Looking back at the highway and watching the cars flash by, I thought of the contrast between the slowness of walking this ancient trail, which of necessity followed the waterways, and the speed of vehicles over modern highways which lead wherever man might wish to go. Earlier, on the trail, I had been convinced that modern means of transportation were best. But now

50

that my breathing was easier, my legs ached less, and my packs seemed lighter, I preferred the ancient mode of travel.

Continuing on slowly we looked for places the voyageurs might have used for *posés*. At these places we envisioned groups of the canoemen sitting on their packs and smoking their pipes as they hurled friendly insults at others on the move, and talked of the ball the evening before.

Where the ninth *posé* would have been, we passed through a beautiful section of the trail. Moss hanging from balsams and cedars gave off a spicy smell. Rose bushes grew along the trail, the brilliant crimson of their fruit accented by the blue of asters scattered among them. In a low place, where reindeer moss clung to flat rocks, we found a small pool of clear spring water. Though water-skaters drew arabesques over its mirror surface, we ignored them and bent to drink.

While we listened to the hammering of a pileated woodpecker a gray, soft, fluffy whisky-jack glided silently in front of us. It reminded me of Bigsby's Whistling John. Writing for friends back home, he said, "It has a long bill, and is almost all feathers. Its back is brown, and breast white. It is extremely familiar, and goes about whistling a little note of its own, seeking small objects, which it hoards. It is of the size of an English blackbird."

We went on until Harvi put the prow of the canoe in the crotch of a small birch. "It's time for another posy."

"I'm too pooped to pick flowers, Harvi," Belva said, squirming out of her pack, "but I could do with another *posé*!" She flopped down with a groan. "Why don't you characters make this trip authentic and carry me pickaback, the way the voyageurs carried the first female travelers across portages?"

"If you put on a skirt and act as demure as they did, maybe we would," I countered.

"Sure could do with a horse about now," said Harvi. He was squatting on his heels with his back resting against the tree.

I looked at him and grinned. "You aren't the first to think of that. The Nor'Westers did too." Mackenzie said, "This is a labour which cattle cannot conveniently perform in summer, as both horses and oxen were tried by the company without success. They are only useful for light, bulky articles; or for transporting upon sledges, during the winter, whatever goods may remain there."

On and on the trail went. I jotted down notes as we threaded our way through the forest: "passed through a grove of cedar with their raked gray bark and spiced, feathery leaves — chickadees all around us, many upside down — aspen now — passed a swamp — inspected the holes and chippings of a pileated woodpecker in the base of an old snag — heard the nasal *yank, yank* of a red-breasted nuthatch — looked in awe at a huge white pine, the tall column of fissured bark led up to whorls of sweeping branches, must have been a seedling when the voyageurs used the portage — crawled under a windfall — air filled with the heady smell of balsam, an odor which epitomizes the north country — uninterrupted silence — thought of the fortunes in furs hauled over the portage — passed some flat rock ledges and some old corduroy — startled by a ruffed grouse as it suddenly whirred up, cracking through the dead branches overhead — swamp — began to climb — inspected a tree trunk, black and scarred from lightning, with small green balsams coming up through a hole in the base — level again — more corduroy — came to a clearing with an old tumbled down cabin on the right — searched for the trail and found it in some bushes on the left — uphill again — red-tailed hawk soaring overhead — feeling of lonesomeness and desolation — legs starting to ache again — uphill and down — will the trail never end? — on and on — trail now forks, a sign on a tree marks the way, right to the cascades, left to Fort Charlotte — passed a few birches large enough to strip for canoes — fresh moose tracks in portage path, judging by the length of his stride, he must have been in a hurry — swamp again — level now and many spruce — can see a break in the trees ahead — now hear rushing water — at last, the river!"

It was 4 P.M. We shed our packs with relief, and followed Harvi down to the bank, watching with satisfaction as he lowered the canoe at the end of the trail.

"Well, we made 'er," he said. "Here's Pigeon River."

What a welcome sight it was! From the bend upstream it flowed with a gentle current between low grassy banks. Downstream the riffles of a small rapid sparkled in the glancing rays of the late afternoon sun. Deep imprints in the mud near shore showed us where the moose whose tracks we had observed all day had crossed from the opposite shore about thirty yards away.

Exhausted, Belva and I dropped down to rest. We fell asleep, and awoke somewhat sheepishly a little later to find that Harvi had put up the tent. The sky was filled with the flush of sunset, and the cool air of night was descending as we built the campfire. Ravenously hungry, we ate supper in silent appreciation.

"No reading tonight," I announced after supper. "I'm too tired."

Belva stretched. "I'm glad. I've had it too. I'm going to bed."

October 3. FORT CHARLOTTE TO THE
MEADOW ON THE PIGEON RIVER

WE AROSE as a hint of light appeared in the east. Rose streamers filled the sky and faded as the sun emerged and warmed the air. We ate breakfast listening to the muted roar of the cascades downstream.

Then we began searching for the ruins of Fort Charlotte, an important North West Company fort used as a depot for trade goods carried across the portage. Here the trade goods remained until the traders were ready to load their canoes and leave for their wintering posts. Named for King George III's queen, Charlotte of Mecklenburg-Strelitz, it had long been in use. Even in 1793, Macdonell wrote: "Mr. Donald Ross has been so long in charge of Fort Charlotte that he has acquired the respectable name of Governor."

Looking about, we could make out only a rectangular grass-grown mound to the south of the portage trail near the river, the only remains of the two enclosures formerly standing here. In 1823, Delafield saw more: "scarcely a trace remaining of its former condition except the cleared ground. A few stumps of burnt pickets assist in tracing the extent of the former enclosures, and that is all." He went on, "It is a pretty place & a profusion of wild roses & the sweet pea and high growth of grass, in the absense of all other considerations, afforded a momentary reconciliation to the spot. . . . The landing place or dock . . . is still entire and affords some accommodation."

54

We wandered downstream to view the cascades. I took our treasured notebooks with us. At the cascades Pigeon River begins a series of spectacular rapids and falls that winds twenty miles through the woods to Lake Superior. It was a beautiful sight, not different from the descriptions given by Bigsby in 1823 and Owen in 1849.

I read first from Bigsby.

"One mile east of us, towards Lake Superior, begins a long and most picturesque series of cascades and rapids, one of the former plunging into a mural chasm 200 feet deep with a gloomy desparation worthy of the Handeck in Switzerland. The sides of the river hereabouts are rocky terraces, naked and high, or are ravines choked with huge *débris* overspread with underwood, wild roses, and raspberries. Its left bank rises to the height of 800 or 900 feet [obviously an error], and has only a few tufts of pines growing in the fissures. It is a very savage place, and will repay a visit. I was almost a whole day in scrambling two miles below the first fall, and returned to camp in a very tattered state.

"The mosquitoes were ferocious, their bites being also much envenomed by our salt diet. Although the heat was very great in these close woods, we wore gloves, veils, and caps over the ears. My pantaloons were tied close down to the boots, or the creatures would have crept up the legs.

"I could not help wishing them to leave me alone, and with Bryant begged them to

> Try some plump alderman, and suck the blood
> Enriched with generous wine and costly meat:
> On well-filled skins fix thy light pump,
> And press thy freckled feet."

"I *like* Bigsby," said Belva. "Now let's hear Owen."

"The scenery at the Cascades presents the singular combination of wild grandeur and picturesque beauty, with an aspect the most dreary and desolate imaginable. In the distance of four hundred yards, the river falls one hundred and forty-four feet. The fall is in a series of cascades through a narrow gorge, with perpendicular walls, varying from forty to one hundred and twenty feet in height, on both sides of the river. The gorge is from fifteen to thirty feet in width, and crooked, presenting numerous angles,

55

around which the foaming waters fret their way with arrowy swiftness, plunging down abrupt slopes, or falling in beautiful cascades."

The description in Owen was actually written by Joseph Norwood, who made the first geological survey of the area as assistant to David Dale Owen.

Loading our canoe back at Fort Charlotte, I could visualize the busy scene here years ago, from the fifteenth of July to the first of August. Then northmen scurried over the dock to load the freshly gummed canoes with packs that the pork-eaters had taken fifteen days to portage and deposit at Fort Charlotte. Clerks barked orders, which the interpreter promptly translated into French for the voyageurs. Finally the loaded north canoes, riding low in the Pigeon River, would start upstream with their voyageurs in full song.

From here on smaller canoes were necessary, for the large Montreal canoes could not be used on the lakes and streams west of Grand Portage. The smaller canoes, known as north canoes, or *canots du nord*, were twenty-five to thirty feet long, and carried about thirty-five *pièces*, of which twenty-three were trade goods, the rest being provisions, stores, and baggage. Manned by six to eight voyageurs, the north canoe was so light it could be portaged upright by two men.

Its crew consisted of a bowsman — *avant de canot*, a steersman — *gouvernail*, and six middlemen — *milieux*. Acting as guide (as well as interpreter), the bowsman sat alone in the bow, using a large paddle for shooting rapids. The steersman, standing in the stern while the canoe was in motion, used a paddle about five inches wide as he steered the craft through raging rapids. The remaining six men sat on three seats, five feet apart, in the middle of the canoe. These *milieux*, or common voyageurs, used paddles four feet long, the blades of which measured two feet in length, three inches in width, and five-eighths inch in breadth at the center. A source of pride to the voyageurs, the paddles were made of cedar, painted red and decorated with black and green.

What a contrast our canoe load would make with that of a north canoe sent out by Alexander Henry the younger as part of a brigade of canoes in 1800. We had a tent, sleeping bags, a large camera case, a small pack for personal belongings, and a food pack. Henry's canoe had "28 *pièces:*

56

Merchandise, 90 pounds each, ...	5 bales
Canal tobacco, ...	1 bale
Kettles, ...	1 bale
Guns, ...	1 case
Iron works, ...	1 case
New twist tobacco, ...	2 rolls
Leaden balls, ...	2 bags
Leaden shot, ...	1 bag
Flour, ...	1 bag
Sugar, ...	1 keg
Gunpowder, ...	2 kegs
High wine, 9 gallons each, ...	10 kegs

plus provisions for four men to Red River — 4 bags of corn; ½ keg grease; and 4 *pièces* of private property belonging to the men."

A nephew of Henry the elder, he became a clerk for the North West Company about 1792, and a partner sometime between 1799 and 1802. Keeping a day-by-day account of his travels, he journeyed throughout the Northwest for twenty-two years as a fur trader, until he drowned in 1814 off Fort George on the Pacific coast.

Formed into brigades of four to eight, the canoes and men were then dispatched in a manner described by David Thompson. "Those for the most Distant Trading Posts were sent off first; with an allowance of two days between each brigade, to prevent incumberances on the Carrying Places." Apparently they had wilderness traffic problems even then!

Dipping my paddle into the muddy water of the river as we started out, I looked around me and thought what a glorious time this was to take a canoe trip. Autumn meant days filled with warmth and softened sunshine; nights cool and frosty, with white mists swirling and running over the lakes in the mornings; portage paths carpets of red and gold, filled with the smell of leaves. It meant grasses, ferns, and weeds varying in color from sienna to bronze and copper; green pine forests tinted with the gold leaves of aspen and birch and the fire of maple; blueberry, honeysuckle, poison ivy, sumac, and Juneberry — all vivid shades of scarlet and gold. And it meant rivers and lakes, unbroken stretches of shimmering blue; indescribable sunrises and sunsets to mark the beginning and ending of each day.

These would be ours, though we would miss summer's smells and sounds and sights, so familiar to the voyageurs: perfume from the pink twin bells of linnea growing among moss and rocks in shady forest depths, the resonant bell note of the hermit thrush penetrating the forest, the piping of frogs in bog and swamp, the satin sheen of blueberries on waxy-leaved shrubs growing on sunny rock shores.

I turned to Harvi and said, "This is Rivière aux Tourtes."

"What?" he asked.

"*Tourtes*. It's probably a corruption of the French *tourterelles*, meaning turtledoves or pigeons," I explained.

The voyageurs gave names to all the lakes and streams and portages. Some they retained from the Chippewa. Others they translated into French from the Indian. But most of the names they made up themselves, usually after some prominent feature or object. Today our names for many of the lakes and streams and portages are derived from those of the voyageurs.

"Too bad all the portages can't be marked with those nice-sounding names," Harvi said. "It would sort of add to the country."

In 1775 Alexander Henry the elder gave the river another name, Aux Groseilles, which, some say, was for Groseilliers who may have visited it with Radisson. More likely it referred to the growth of wild gooseberries on its banks. The more recent name, Pigeon, probably referred to the large flocks of the now extinct passenger pigeons found flying about it.

"I can't see," Belva complained. "What do you think I am, just some of the bag — I mean luggage?"

After we shifted the packs in the canoe so she could see better, everybody was happy. Then we broke the silence with a favorite voyageurs' song, "En roulant ma boule roulant."

> Three bonnie ducks go swimming 'round,
> On, roll on my ball, on!
> The prince goes off a-hunting bound,
> Roll on, my ball, my ball I roll on.
> On, roll on, my ball I roll on,
> On, roll on my ball, on!

The voyageurs sang of their daily adventures, their loves, their surroundings, and life and death itself. Sung to lighten the work, their paddling songs, or *chansons de voyageur*, were spontaneous and ephemeral, useful only for the instant, but escaping definition because of their variable content. The tempo of these *chansons à l'aviron* was adapted to the speed of their flashing red paddles. Usually the steersman chose the phrase which the others would pick up as the chorus. This they would repeat again and again, as the steersman developed and embroidered on the original idea. The song, floating over the lakes, among the islands, and into the forest, lasted the whole course of the lake or stream they paddled over, and usually ended with a piercing Indian cry. Some of these became favorites, on repetition, and then were sung in chorus by the entire crew.

At night around the campfire, they sang their *complaintes*, or lyrical poems. Composed about their lives and loves, the poems were extravagant with pathos and romance. Like songs sung by any band of men away from home, they told of unrequited love or tragic events. Some gave advice with moral undertones.

I am sure the voyageurs would have ridiculed our singing, but we tried anyway.

A short paddle brought us to a falls, the first obstruction to navigation, and Partridge portage (Portage du Perdrix). It is a "tolerable good Carrying Place" as David Thompson would say, about seventy rods to the left of the falls. Here the river pours with a roar in three perpendicular cascades, about forty feet in all, over the first outcropping of rock since Fort Charlotte.

On this portage in 1802 an amusing incident occurred, one of many in the rivalry between the North West and XY Companies. George Nelson, a Pottie, recalled it. "One of our brigades . . . slept . . . at Portage la Perdrix, only a few hundred yards from our Stores at the north end of the Grand Portage [the XY Company had a post near Fort Charlotte], where they feasted & got drunk upon the 'régale' that was always given them when they arrived from, or departed for, their winter quarters. When they arose the next morning they found thirty Kegs of High Wines (containing 9 Galls. ea.) had all run out! Upon examination it was found that they had been bored with two gimlets holes each! The consternation & injury this occasioned may be imagined. Enquiries were set on foot & affidavits given in. No bible was to be found to swear upon. I lent mine, for the purpose, but never saw it after though I enquired diligently. These were called *witty tricks*. Rumor gave out that it was Benjamin Frobisher [a prominent Nor' Wester] & [——] who bored the Kegs."

Crossing the portage with ease, we proceeded upstream two and a half miles and came to the Meadow — La Prairie, the voyageurs usual first camping ground.

Here Alexander Henry the younger wrote: "All were merry over their favorite regale [high wine], which is always given on their departure [from Fort Charlotte], and generally enjoyed at this spot, where we have a delightful meadow to pitch our tents, and plenty of elbow-room for the men's antics."

It was only two in the afternoon, but we decided to go no further as our backs and shoulders still ached from yesterday's labor. After a short rest we made our camp in a grassy spot, and enjoyed the place almost as much as the voyageurs had.

Now the grass was full grown. In those days it was cut to make camping and frolicking easier. David Thompson wrote, "Come to the Prairie at 6:20 P.M. and put up. Found a very small stack of Hay. A good deal of the grass left unmowed."

Although the grass was uncut, we at least did not have to cope with mosquitoes as they did. Bigsby complained, "The mosquitoes were in billions. As soon as the tread of man gave notice of his approach, I saw them rising to the feast in clouds out of the coarse grass around. We burnt the grass after watering it, and lived in the smoke."

After the Meadow there would be no more feasting for the voyageurs, only lyed corn and grease until they reached Bas de la Rivière, at the mouth of the Winnipeg River, where pemmican would be distributed to them. Occasionally, time and circumstances permitting, berries, game, or fish relieved the monotony of their diet.

Mackenzie told how the voyageurs' corn-and-grease mixture was prepared: "One quart of this [lyed corn] is boiled for two hours, over a moderate fire, in a gallon of water; to which, when it has boiled a small time, are added two ounces of melted suet; this causes the corn to split, and in the time mentioned makes a pretty thick pudding. If to this is added a little salt, (but not before it is boiled, as it would interrupt the operation) it makes an wholesome, palatable food, and easy of digestion. This quantity is fully sufficient for a man's subsistence during twenty-four hours."

Then in a circle around the kettle filled with the thick white mass, the voyageurs would speedily empty it with their wooden spoons. After a pipe they would fall asleep on a bed of marsh hay, much as we did this night.

October 4. FROM THE
MEADOW TO MOUNTAIN LAKE

Our aches and pains were almost gone this morning, and we had a full day of canoeing ahead. How we looked forward to it! We proceeded to Big Rock, or Great Stone portage (Portage Grosse Roche), which is a mile and a half from the Meadow. It is on the right side of the river, about ninety rods long, and passes over a very low ridge.

A short distance from here, Caribou or Deer portage (Portage Carreboeuf) follows, on the left, a hundred rods long.

From the Meadow to Caribou portage, the river became so shallow that we were forced to learn first hand what the voyageurs meant by a *décharge*. This was a lazy man's way of not making a portage (or would it be a smart man's way?). A *décharge* was made whenever an obstacle was encountered which was not great enough to require a portage. In these places the canoe could be towed through shallow or rapid water with all or part of its cargo included. The voyageurs would either pull the canoe with a rope from shore, or wade through the cold water, knee- to waist-deep, over slippery rocks, pulling the canoe with them.

We *décharged* all the way to Caribou portage!

Mackenzie described how the voyageurs proceeded from the Meadow to Caribou portage "when half the lading is taken out, and carried by part of the crew, while two of them are conducting the canoe among the rocks, with the remainder, to the Carreboeuf Portage, three miles and an half more, when they unload and come back two miles, and embark what was left for the other hands to carry, which they also land with the former; all of which is carried six hundred and eighty paces, and the canoe led up against the rapid."

Three miles from Caribou portage we finally came to Bustard, Fowl, or Goose Portage (Portage aux Outardes), probably named after the Canada goose. After Caribou portage the water became deeper, so the going was easier.

From Big Rock to Fowl portage the river is bordered on both sides by extensive swamps which, on the American side, extend back to ridges. The portage, in poor condition, passes over low ridges for three hundred and twenty rods. Belva got out of the canoe and glared at the portage, mumbling something about canoeing all day before she disgustedly lifted her pack and started over the trail.

So after much labor, sweat, and fatigue, we arrived at South Fowl Lake (Lac aux Outardes) greatly relieved to have the Pigeon River behind us. Now the lakes along the border would rapidly reveal themselves, and we could really enjoy the scenery.

The trip up the Pigeon River was hard enough with nothing but natural obstacles. Imagine making the trip with manmade obstructions added! One poor trader in 1806 had to make the river trip under just those circumstances. Lord Selkirk told of his fate: "Mr. Delorme proceeded (with two loaded canoes) as far as Lake Superior, and, in order to avoid collision, he there took the old route by the Grand Portage, which the Northwest Company had then abandoned. When he advanced a few days' journey through the intricate and difficult country beyond Lake Superior, he was overtaken by Mr. Alexander McKay, a partner of the Northwest Company, with a number of men, who went forward along the route, by which Mr. Delorme was to advance, and proceeded to fell trees across the road, at the portages, and on all the narrow creeks by which they were to pass. They soon accomplished such a complete obstruction, that Mr. Delorme with his small party, found it impossible to open a passage for his loaded canoes. His adventure being thus entirely frustrated, he left his goods, and made his retreat with his men only."

At the end of the portage stands Goose Rock, guarding the exit of the lake. Because it is a hill 350 feet high, we debated whether or not to climb it, deciding finally that it would be easier to read Bigsby, who *had* climbed it. "The view from the summit is beautiful. A strong north-west gale was blowing across a clear sky successive companies of clouds, which mapped the sea of woods before me with fugitive shadows. Looking to the north-west, Lake Outard lay below, nearly bisected by a rushy narrow. Beyond it we have hilly ranges of woods, running W.N.W., with long valleys between. To the south and south-east we see the valley of Pigeon River buried in dark pines, among which we still discern short silvery traces of the stream itself."

We paddled over the clear green waters of South Fowl Lake, admiring the surrounding highlands which are broken by valleys every mile or so. The Fowl Lakes, North and South together, are about four miles in length and one or two miles wide. Formerly the two lakes were separated by a small stream running through rushes, but are now one lake.

As we stopped to rest, Belva asked, "Is this the place where Bigsby says Lord Selkirk tried to start an agricultural community?"

I nodded.

"What a Godforsaken place," she grimaced. "I can understand why it failed."

Soon the canoe was mired in mud at the west end of the lake. "Well, here we are at the portage," Harvi said as he stood up to survey the shore.

Moose portage (Portage Orignal) follows the north side of a small stream. It was a difficult one. We struggled with dead snags while floundering knee-deep in muck, then forced our way through dense grass and brush to the path, which was a hellish jumble of sharp-edged pieces of slate. Our troubles ended abruptly near the end of the portage. Through the birches bordering the trail, we looked out on the peaceful water of Moose Lake.

From here to Gunflint the lakes we were to pass through are similar, generally long and narrow and with water of clear green. They are surrounded by high jagged hills which rise sharply on the north and then slope gently away on the south, giving them a sawtooth topography. Geologists tell us that erosion has carved out the slate which underlies the region, leaving valleys, while the resistant diabase sills intruded into the slate re-

64

main as asymmetrical ridges. Glacial gouging and deposit have resulted in many longitudinal depressions in the valleys — depressions which have filled with water.

As we started across Moose Lake (Lac Orignal), I thought what a desolate place it must have been to spend a winter. But the Hudson's Bay Company traders in the middle of the nineteenth century probably did not mind their lonely stay here. I looked for the likely location of their house and decided it must have been on a flat ledge of rock close to the portage on the Canadian side.

I stared at the small clearing, trying to picture it as it must have been one hundred years ago in the winter. I could imagine a waterhole in the ice near shore. From it a narrow path led through deep snow to a picketed stockade in a clearing on the edge of the dark pine forest. Smoke slowly curled upward from the clay and stone chimney of one of the two small log cabins inside the enclosure and then hovered in layers in the below-zero air. Snow lay in deep drifts against the walls of the stockade and around the buildings. Inside one of the cabins, kept unheated to prevent spoilage, stacks of prime beaver blankets, *pièces* of trade goods, and food supplies lay scattered about the room. In the other cabin soft light filtered through the oiled deerskin window to reveal the dwelling's crude furniture — a double wall bunk and, opposite, a table and stools. The flickering light of the fire fell on snowshoes and guns hanging on the wall, and paddles standing in the corner.

As we continued through Moose Lake a solitary gull, sitting in the very middle of the large expanse, emphasized the lake's loneliness. We admired the region's high escarpments and stands of young aspen and birch. The forests of Moose Lake, along with those of the other eastern lakes, were scarred and blackened by fires which raged through them in the dry summer of 1936. Now the once-barren shores are covered with the gold of aspen and birch. Here and there a splash of green marks where young spruce and pine are effecting the final step toward the restoration of these forests.

These cycles of destruction by fire and regrowth went on in ages past, too. In 1735, Father Aulneau, the second Jesuit missionary to serve at Fort St. Charles, traversed these same lakes and streams from Lake Superior to Lake of the Woods "through fire and a thick stifling smoke, which prevented us from even once catching a glimpse of the sun."

Through the entire four miles of the lake we searched its south shore, wondering where the Cleveland Fur Company could have put a house in 1844. Still undecided, we came to Long or Great Cherry portage (Grand Portage des Cerises).

Harvi started up the portage path with the unloaded canoe. Belva and I followed with the packs. A few hundred feet up the trail Belva stopped. "Listen, Arnold. Did you ever hear such a cheerfully busy sound?"

Through the trees we could see, alongside the path, an ambitious little stream hubbubbling down the hill. It boiled around boulders and wrestled with fallen trees until it pushed itself over a ledge with a triumphant shout into a frothy pool of exhaustion. Slowly it collected itself, flexing in ever-widening eddies, then stretched out, leisurely seeking the sunflecked expanse of Moose Lake.

We followed the path beside the creek 146 rods northwest over sharp stones to Lower Lily Lake (Lac Vaseux). It was a small, shallow, muddy pond about a mile long, covered with bronze lily pads and bordered with saffron-yellow reeds, marsh grass, and wild rice.

"Smell the marsh grass — and listen: I hear mallards quacking," Belva said, as we started over Lower Lily Lake. Just then two mallards startled us as they flew up from the rice beds. The autumn sunshine sparkled on the water dripping from their webbed feet and glinted on the iridescence of their green heads and purple wing bars. They climbed high and swung south, slowly disappearing from view.

We portaged Little Muddy or second Cherry portage (Portage Petit Vaseux) to Upper Lily Lake.

As I dropped my packs at the end of the portage, something moved in the distance across the pond. I reached for my glasses and focused them quickly. It was a moose! He stood in some pond weeds and lily pads staring in my direction, with water dribbling from his incongruous muzzle. I stood looking at his broad antlers, humpback, and the whole unbelievable bulk of him, until he turned and awkwardly loped into the woods. I wished Belva and Harvi could have seen him, but they were just a little too late.

Crossing Upper Lily Lake, about a half mile long, we came to the third

66

Little or Lesser Cherry portage (Portage Petit Vaseux). It is a portage of fifty rods along the side of a high rock cliff, through a thick grove of cedar to a little bay at the outlet of Mountain Lake (Lac de la Montaigne).

At the end of the portage we pitched our tent on a level spot sheltered by balsams, and soon had a fire going. During supper we watched the sun settle behind a pink fluff of clouds low on the horizon, edging them in silver. The eastern sky turned slate gray. Sitting down beside the fire a little later, Belva sipped her coffee and asked, "What'll we read tonight?"

"Tanner," I answered.

"Who's he?" Harvi asked.

"A white boy who was captured by the Indians," I told him. "He spent part of the summer and fall of 1793 at Moose Lake on his first trip through the border country."

Captured by two Shawnees who abducted him while he was gathering hickory nuts at the edge of a clearing near his home in Ohio, John Tanner was traded for ten gallons of whiskey to a Chippewa woman, Net-no-kwa, with whom he went to live in the Red River and Assiniboine valleys. After roaming the Quetico-Superior and adjoining country for thirty years as an Indian, he dictated his experiences to Edwin James, the army surgeon at Fort Brady, Sault Ste. Marie, who published them in 1830. Through the book's pages we may relive his experiences as an Indian on border waters during the period of the fur trade. I moved closer to the yellow light of our fire to read from my notes about Tanner and his Indian family.

"When we came to the Saut of St. Marie, we put all our baggage on board the trader's vessel, which was about to sail to the upper end of Lake Superior, and went on ourselves in our canoes. The winds were light, which enabled us to run faster than the vessel, and we arrived ten days before it, at the Portage [Grand Portage]. When she at last came, and anchored out at a little distance from the shore, my father and his two sons, Wa-me-gon-a-biew, (he who puts on feathers,) the eldest, and Ke-wa-tin, (the north wind,) went out in a canoe to get the baggage. In jumping down into the hold of the vessel, the younger of these young men fell with his knee upon a knot of the rope tied around a bundle of goods, and received an injury from which he never recovered. The same night his knee was

67

badly swollen, and on the next day he was not able to go out of the lodge. After about eight or ten days, we commenced crossing the Grand Portage: we carried him on our shoulders, by fastening a blanket to two poles; but he was so sick that we had to stop often, which made us long in passing. We left our canoes at the trading-house, and when we came to the other side of the Portage, were detained some days to make small canoes. When these were nearly finished, my father sent me, with one of his wives, back to the trading-house, to bring something which had been forgotten. On our return, we met the two boys at some distance, coming to tell me to hasten home, for my father was dying, and he wished to see me before he died. When I came into the lodge, I found that he was indeed dying, and though he could see, he was not able to speak to me. In a few minutes he ceased to breathe. Beside him lay the gun which he had taken in his hand a few minutes before, to shoot the young man who had wounded him at Mackinac. . . . The old woman procured a coffin from the traders, and they brought my father's body, in a wagon, to the trading house, on this side the Grand Portage, where they buried him, in the burying ground of the whites. His two sons, as well as the young man who killed him, accompanied his body to the Portage. This last was near being killed by one of my brothers; but the other prevented him, as he was about to strike.

"It was but a very short time after my father died, that we started on our journey to Red River. My brother Ke-wa-tin we carried on a litter, as we had done before, whenever it was necessary to take him out of the canoe. We had passed two carrying places, and arrived at the third, called the Moose carrying place, when he said to us, 'I must die here; I cannot go farther.' So Net-no-kwa determined to stop here, and the remainder of the party went on. A part of our own family chose to continue on with those going to Red River. So that, after they had started, there remained only the old woman, and one of the younger wives of Tau-ga-we-ninne, Wa-me-gon-a-biew, the elder brother, Ke-wa-tin, the second, and myself, the youngest. It was about the middle of summer, for the small berries were ripe, when we stopped here on the borders of Moose Lake, which is of cool and clear water, like Lake Superior. It is small and round, and a canoe can be very plainly seen across the widest part of it. We were only two of us able to do any thing; and being myself very young, and without any experience as a hunter, we had apprehension that, being left thus alone, we might soon be in want. We had brought with us one of the nets used about Mackinac, and setting this, the first night, caught about eighty trout and white fish. After remaining here some time, we found beavers, of which we killed six; also, some otters and muskrats. We had brought with us some corn and grease, so that, with the fish we caught, and the game we killed, we lived comfortably. But, at the approach of winter, the old woman told us she could not venture to remain there by herself, as the winter would be long and cold, and no people, either whites or Indians, near us. Ke-wa-tin was now so sick and weak, that in going back to the Portage, we were compelled to move slowly; and when we arrived, the waters were beginning to freeze. He lived but a month or two after we arrived. It must have been in the early part, or before the middle of winter, that he died. The old woman buried him by the side of her husband, and hung up one of her flags at his grave.

"We now, as the weather became severe, began to grow poor, Wa-me-gon-a-biew and myself being unable to kill as much game as we wanted. He was seventeen years of age, and I thirteen, and game was not plentiful. As the weather became more and more cold, we removed from the trading house, and set up our lodge in the woods, that we might get wood easier. Here my brother and myself had to exert ourselves to the utmost, to avoid starving. We used to hunt two or three days' distance from home, and often returned with but little meat. We had, on one of our hunting paths, a camp built of cedar boughs, in which we had kindled fire so often, that at length it became very dry, and at last caught fire as we were lying in it. The cedar had become so dry that it flashed up like powder, but fortunately we escaped with little injury. As we were returning, and still a great distance from home, we attempted to cross a river which was so rapid as never to freeze very sound. Though the weather was so cold that the trees were constantly cracking with the frost, we broke in, I first, and afterwards my brother; and he, in attempting to throw himself down upon the ice, wet himself nearly all over, while I had at first only my feet and legs wet. Owing to our hands being benumbed with the cold, it was long before we could extricate ourselves from our snow shoes, and we were no sooner out of the water, than our moccasins and leggins were frozen stiff.

69

My brother was soon discouraged, and said he was willing to die. Our spunk wood had got wet when we fell in, and though we at length reached the shore, as we were unable to raise a fire, and our moccasins and cloathes were frozen so stiff that we could not travel, I began also to think that we must die. But I was not like my Indian brother, willing to sit down and wait patiently for death to come. I kept moving about to the best of my power, while he lay in a dry place by the side of the bank, where the wind had blown away the snow. I at length found some very dry rotten wood, which I used as a substitute for spunk, and was so happy as to raise a fire. We then applied ourselves to thaw and dry our moccasins, and when partly dry we put them on, and went to collect fuel for a larger fire than we had before been able to make. At length, when night came on, we had a comfortable fire and dry cloathes, and though we had nothing to eat, we did not regard this, after the more severe suffering from cold. At the earliest dawn we left our camp, and proceeded towards home; but at no great distance met our mother, bringing dry clothes and a little food. She knew that we ought to have been home on the preceding day by sun set, and was also aware of the difficult river we had to cross. Soon after dark, being convinced that we must have fallen through the ice, she started, and walking all night, met us not far from the place where the accident happened.

"Thus we lived for some time, in a suffering and almost starving condition."

As I finished reading, Belva, chin on hand, thought out loud. "Yup, that was the Chippewa all right. He was either starving or feasting."

"That's right," I agreed. "Parkman, the historian, described them well. Read what he said." I handed her the notebook.

"In the calm days of summer, the Ojibwa fisherman pushes out his birch canoe upon the great inland ocean of the north; and as he gazes down into the pellucid depths, he seems like one balanced between earth and sky. The watchful fish-hawk circles above his head; and below, farther than his line will reach, he sees the trout glide shadowy and silent over the glimmering pebbles. The little islands on the verge of the horizon seem now starting into spires, now melting from the sight, now shaping themselves into a thousand fantastic forms, with the strange mirage of the waters; and he fancies that the evil spirits of the lake lie basking their serpent forms on

70

those unhallowed shores. Again, he explores the watery labyrinths where the stream sweeps among pine-tufted islands, or runs, black and deep, beneath the shadows of moss-bearded firs; or he lifts his canoe upon the sandy beach, and, while his camp-fire crackles on the grass plat, reclines beneath the trees, and smokes and laughs away the sultry hours, in a lazy luxury of enjoyment.

"But when winter descends upon the north, sealing up the fountains, fettering the streams, and turning the greenrobed forests to shivering nakedness, then, bearing their frail dwellings on their backs, the Ojibwa family wander forth into the wilderness, cheered only, on their dreary track, by the whistling of the north wind, and the hungry howl of wolves. By the banks of some frozen stream, women and children, men and dogs, lie crouched together around the fire. They spread their benumbed fingers over the embers, while the wind shrieks through the fir trees like the gale through the rigging of a frigate, and the narrow concave of the wigwam sparkles with the frost-work of their congealed breath. In vain they beat the magic drum, and call upon their guardian manitoes; — the wary moose keeps aloof, the bear lies close in his hollow tree, and famine stares them in the face. And now the hunter can fight no more against the nipping cold and blinding sleet. Stiff and stark, with haggard cheek and shrivelled lip, he lies among the snow-drifts; till with tooth and claw, the famished wild-cat strives in vain to pierce the frigid marble of his limbs. Such harsh schooling is thrown away on the incorrigible mind of the northern Algonquin. He lives in misery, as his fathers lived before him. Still, in the brief hour of plenty, he forgets the season of want; and still the sleet and the snow descend upon his houseless head."

We fell asleep early, but the muffled thump, thump, thump of a silly grouse drumming nearby awakened us several times during the night. How futile his labors were at this time of the year! Once when he woke us, we heard some tiny woods creatures scampering and sliding on our upturned canoe. After a resounding *bon-n-n-g* as the metal contracted in the cold night, the silence that followed was almost tangible. We lay listening, and finally heard our small friends resume their nocturnal frolic, cautiously at first, then in complete abandon.

71

October 5

MOUNTAIN LAKE TO ROSE LAKE

Nᴇxᴛ morning, while eating breakfast, I looked across Mountain Lake, shining like a giant emerald in the bright morning sun. Called *Keesh-ku-te-na* by the Chippewa, it lies nearly east and west, six miles long and two miles wide. On its south shore are chains of high hills or mountains alternating with valleys; its north shore is rather low, except for a high ridge running along the northwest extent of a deep bay.

Just as we were ready to leave, Belva went down to the lake for a drink. Rising from her knees on the shore, she suddenly ducked. A kingfisher, flashing bright blue in the early morning sun, swooped over her with a rackety, bantering call. She straightened to watch him. Then down she went again. A second one noisily rocketed past her and after the other. Up and down, across and around the little bay they chased in a zany game of

72

tag. I laughed out loud as I watched. Flinching in the ricochet of birds and chatter, Belva cheered them on until they darted like jolly blue banshees out over the lake.

"Let's shove off." Harvi had the canoe loaded and waiting.

We started into the sunlit cloudless day, eager to reach the Quetico-Superior country. In high spirits I said to Harvi, "Let's see how fast and how far we can paddle."

Harvi looked puzzled. "I don't see why, but if you want to, OK."

Off we spurted, but it didn't last long.

"You'd sure make fine voyageurs!" Belva scoffed. "Only ten minutes of paddling. I'm not very proud of you."

"Shush, woman. How else can Harvi appreciate the speed and endurance of the voyageurs?"

The voyageurs' abilities were best shown in the grueling races they held on Lake Winnipeg on their way to the Northwest. These races came about when the haughty Athabaskans hurled insults at northmen in other brigades crossing the lake. The gibes always had the desired effect. No man, Athabaskans included, could poke fun at any northman. Tempers flared. Then the race started. Incredible as it sounds, they would paddle forty hours without stopping, sixty strokes a minute, until ordered to halt, or until one group dropped with exhaustion.

As we drifted on the lake, resting, I looked north to the bay, where a variation of our route led by difficult portages to Arrow Lake, and rejoined ours ahead at Rose Lake.

Heading for the notch on the horizon we came to Watab portage (Portage Petit Neuf). It was designated "new" when the Nor'Westers began using it in preference to the old Arrow Lake route. A good portage of a hundred rods with few obstacles, it follows a ridge to Watab Lake. This lake joins Rove Lake beyond, through a small strait. The two lakes together are three miles long.

Crossing Watab we followed the high ridge on its south shore to the detroit, where the ridge ends in a magnificent escarpment whose slopes hold slides of rock debris. Near the detroit a slowly undulating V of geese came out of the north. The thrilling cadence of their wild honking cries rose and fell in rhythm with their heavy, powerful surge through the warm autumn air. As they passed with necks outstretched, low over the canoe, the sun revealed white patches on the sides of their black heads and highlighted the beat of their wings. Their crying softened and died as they vanished into the southern sky. We wished them well, and started on our way through the narrow passage to Rove Lake.

Henry the younger described "the Petit Détroit, a narrow place where a canoe can scarcely pass. Here, in forcing our passage, we broke a hole in the bottom of one canoe, which obliged us to unload and repair."

Soon we came to the end of the lake and the start of the New Long portage (Grand Portage Neuf). The canoe slipped through sun-dried grasses near the shore. We jumped out into the shallow water and unloaded the packs. As Belva and I started across the portage, we heard the soft scuttering noises of mallards feeding and conversing in a beaver pond nearby.

Up the trail a short way, we were stopped by a barrage of bizarre noises — squeals, squeaks, grunts, and moans. Our curiosity drew us cautiously through the brush and marsh grass to the edge of the pond. Not knowing what to expect, we stopped and peered through a clump of tall cattails. We were dumbfounded to see four beavers noisily enjoying themselves in the quiet water. Ignoring us, though they must have known we were there, they swam and dived, slapping their tails as though having fun. One fat lazy fellow flopped over on his back, scratched his belly, and then reached leisurely for a tasty aspen tidbit. Nowhere had we heard or read of their vocal abilities or playfulness, so we watched them as long as we could, then hurried to catch up with Harvi.

We walked through alternating pools of shade and sunshine. Slender spears of light probed the overhanging branches and, slanting through the tall columns of pine, dappled the unending trail. The path led over sharp rocks, around hummocks, through wet places, over windfalls and tangled roots, up steep ridges and down. We eventually reached an old logging railroad grade which followed the portage to Rose Lake.

"Never have I made a portage as rough as this one," Belva panted, as she leaned against a tree to rest her back. "But then Mackenzie promised us that."

74

He wrote the portage is "over very rough ground, which requires the utmost exertions of the men, and frequently lames them."

Even though the portage crippled some of them, the voyageurs made the best of it. Alexander Henry the younger described his crossing. "The men were early at work on the portage . . . at ten o'clock all was over. Here I found many canoes, some finishing the portage, others embarking; all was bustle and confusion. We pitched our tent for the night, to await the brigade, which arrived this evening. They all made merry upon some small kegs of wine generally given them on their engagement at Grand Portage, one or two gallons to each man."

I sat down to rest at the base of a tall Norway, my head against its crisp surface. Reaching back, I loosened a scale of the bark and admired the silver-edged bit of tarnished copper before snapping it between my fingers. My eyes followed the stately column of its trunk, up and up to the graceful spread of the curved branches. Listening to the faint whisper of the green needle brushes as they swept ever-changing turquoise patterns in the sky, I fell asleep.

Awaking refreshed from my short nap, I heard a hissing sound behind me, and turned quietly to see a male ruffed grouse in full courtship display. He was a shimmering tawny fluff of feathered ecstasy. With his black-banded tail full fanned and black velvet ruff aquiver, he danced an enraptured minuet. I must have startled him, for he sprang up with a whir of wings and disappeared into some pine branches.

As Belva and I started over the last section of the portage, I wished that La Vérendrye had used this portage instead of the Arrow Lake route. In 1734 Beauharnois, governor of Canada, reported that "he has made his hired men work on the trails of his portages and has thus made them so fine and so easy that there is no difficulty in making seven a day."

A mile from Rose Lake the creek we had been following enlarged to a huge pond. We had to load the canoe and pole for a quarter mile across it. "This is a new one," Belva said. "I've never had to ferry over a portage before."

At the end of the pond we saw the reason for our difficulties: a most expertly constructed beaver dam. Through its chinks small streams of water trickled down into the creekbed. I looked back. A handsome bachelor beaver — at least that's what Harvi said he was — dived and splashed near the dam. Behind him on shore, a stand of chalk-white canoe birch stood silhouetted against the blue sky.

How important the beaver and birches had been to the fur trade — yes, and to exploration too! Without birchbark to make canoes for transportation and beaver pelts to meet the demand for hats in Europe, there would have been no traders or explorers and no voyageurs either. But birch and beaver were only part of the story. Other elements were essential too: the Indian demanding the white man's goods, the buffalo to supply pemmican for the long treks into the north, and the waterways of the Canadian shield. How different our history would be were it not for all these.

Harvi started up the trail. "Let's finish the portage," he said, glancing at me from under the canoe.

"We can't have too much farther to go," I reasoned.

"I hope not. Wonder if anyone ever measured the portage."

"David Thompson did," Belva informed him.

It was hard to picture David Thompson stepping off the rough, uneven ground on this portage. But he did, every diabolical yard. And precise as always, he found it to be exactly 2,173 yards long.

Finally we came to its end and looked over Rose Lake (Lac Roseau). Known sometimes as Muddy Lake, its name is a corruption of the French *roseau*, meaning reeds, which commonly grow in a muddy lake. The lake has other names too. *Ka-ba-gouish-ke-wa-ga Saga-ai-gon*, the Chippewa called it; the voyageurs named it Small Fish Lake from the quantity of suckers found in it.

"I'd like to camp over there," Belva said, pointing to a level point of rock directly across the bay.

As we crossed the short distance to Belva's proposed campsite, Harvi said uneasily, "Sure hope we don't get any of that." He pointed to a deep purple thunderhead piled high in the southwest, black sheets of rain slanting down from it. Jagged streaks of lightning hurled from the thunderhead, followed by rolling peals of thunder.

Happily, it passed around us to the south. Even though it didn't drench us, the storm accomplished something. Our camp was made in no time at all. It looked like it, too!

76

"I'm tired," Belva complained after supper. "How about just a short reading tonight?"

Harvi agreed. "I don't even feel like doing the dishes. Let's leave them 'til morning."

As the flush of sunset suffused the lake and its pine shores with a rosy glow, I read a comment from Delafield about a task the voyageurs performed at the end of the New Long portage.

"At the W. end of this portage [New Long portage, which we had just finished], it is usual to prepare the canoe for the descent of rapids, the other side of Height of Land [a portage we soon will make]. This refitting consists in driving the boards or ribs of the canoe, called by the Canadians verons, tight, so that they have a uniform and close bearing upon the bottom or bark. The operation takes two or three hours. The improvement of the canoe is manifest both in firmness and form. The afternoon is most favorable for the voyage and this delay, created as it seem'd, by the Frenchmen, annoyed me very much. Satisfied however that they were exercising their best judgment, and well knowing that everything goes wrong when they are not permitted to be lords of the canoe & the portages, I did not interfere. It would have been fatal to all peace or comfort for a few days at least to have counteracted their plans for their darling canoe. Pride, self-will and obstinancy are virtues with the Canadian in many matters. As an instance, they had alarmed me on account of provisions. Fearing from their gluttony I should fall short, I put them upon rations & constant grumbling & discontent was the consequence. When secure of a supply I allowed them to help themselves, and they actually ate less, traveled farther, and were better-tempered animals for the change."

"Gee, we must be in for some rough waters ahead," Belva commented when I had finished. "Where *do* we go tomorrow?"

Opening the map, we traced our course by the firelight. Tomorrow we would make Saganaga.

October 6. ROSE LAKE TO LAKE SAGANAGA

AFTER washing the supper dishes, eating breakfast, and washing the dishes again, we started on our way.

The sky was dull. A chill was on the lake. We paddled hard waiting for the sun to come up and warm us, but there was another reason too: we were eager to reach our favorite canoe country, the Quetico-Superior, and glad to leave this monotonous sequence of lakes and portages. The long expanses of water in the eastern lakes, interrupted neither by islands nor deceptive bays, and the absence of challenging rivers, made this route the one favored by the voyageurs, whose only concern was easy travel.

Though beautiful and wild in its own right, the country we were passing through seemed to us desolate and unfriendly. Even the diarists said little about it, as if verifying our feelings.

Paddling fast across the six miles of Rose Lake, we soon left its fire-scarred shores and huge escarpment behind and came to Rat portage (Portage la Marte). We portaged the four rods over a high rocky ridge to

Rat Lake. Lac la Marte, as the voyageurs called it, is a shallow little pond of clear water encircled by reeds.

As we started across it, I warned Harvi, "Better be careful. We might be swallowed up in this little puddle."

Looking puzzled, he shrugged his shoulders and put down his paddle. "What the heck do you mean?"

So I read him what Mackenzie had written about the little lake: "the bottom is mud and slime, with about three or four feet of water over it; and here I frequently struck a canoe pole of twelve feet long, without meeting any other obstruction than if the whole were water: It has, however, a peculiar suction or attractive power, so that it is difficult to paddle a canoe over it. There is a small space along the South shore, where the water is deep, and this effect is not felt. In proportion to the distance from this part, the suction becomes more powerful: I have, indeed been told that loaded canoes have been in danger of being swallowed up, and have only owed their preservation to other canoes, which were lighter. I have, myself, found it very difficult to get away from this attractive power, with six men, and great exertion, though they did not appear to be in any danger of sinking."

When I had finished, Harvi headed straight for the danger area, instead of following the south shore.

"Phooey!" He laughed with confidence. "That's just the back pressure that builds up in all shallow waters with muddy bottoms."

The canoe *did* seem to be held back, or I imagined it was. But we reached South Lake portage (Portage les Perches).

After winding over its fifty-seven-rod trail through a beautiful cedar swamp, we came to South Lake (Lac les Perches) or *A-ja-wa-wan Saga-ai-gon* in Chippewa, meaning Lake of the Height of Land.

We crossed over South Lake to an inlet in the northwest point of the lake and Height of Land portage (Portage du Hauteur des Terres).

It was on South Lake, in 1798, that the Indians told Roderick Mc-Kenzie about the Kaministikwia route west of Lake Superior. This road, the alternative water route to our present one, had long been forgotten by the traders after it was first used by the French. Returning to Lac la Croix, McKenzie ascended the Maligne River and followed the route east to the

79

mouth of the Kaministikwia River on Lake Superior. From there he made his way to the annual meeting at Grand Portage with the good news. Steps were soon taken to remove the North West Company establishment from Grand Portage, then on American soil, to the mouth of the Kaministikwia, where Fort William was built.

Height of Land portage, eight rods long and at no point more than twenty feet above water level, follows a valley which cuts through a high ridge ranging northeast and southwest.

After we had landed and unloaded the canoe, I stretched, feeling wonderful for no reason whatsoever. It was a lazy Indian-summer kind of feeling that comes with a day like this — recalling the richness of pumpkin pie, all spicy and warm and mellow.

After lunch I lay back on the grassy bank. A smoky autumn haze veiled the distant shore. The saffron leaves of birches along the trail rustled and trembled in the soft breeze and then spiraled down.

"This is where we become true *hommes du nord*," I announced.

"What's that?" asked Harvi.

"Men of the north," I told him.

"I beg your pardon," Belva said indignantly, "*femme du nord* for me."

It was on this portage that a famous voyageur ceremony took place for all newcomers crossing over into the waters of the Northwest. As men ceremoniously observe decisive crossings of water elsewhere, so it was here. To explain the initiation to Harvi, I read Macdonell's description of the custom. "Passed the Martes, les Perches and Slept at the height of Land, where I was instituted a *North man* by *Batême* performed by sprinkling water in my face with a small cedar Bow dipped in a ditch of water and accepting certain conditions such as not to let any new hand pass by that road without experiencing the same ceremony which stipulates particularly never to kiss a voyageur's wife against her own free will the whole being accompanied by a dozen of Gun shots fired one after another in an Indian manner. The intention of this Batême being only to claim a glass. I complied with the custom and gave the men . . . a two gallon keg as my worthy Bourgeois Mr Cuthbert Grant directed me."

Now, kneeling to repeat the ceremony, each of us, in turn, was sprinkled with water from a cedar branch and "regaled" in voyageur fashion. Harvi, in true voyageur spirit, heartily endorsed the last part of the ceremony at least.

"*Je suis une femme du nord* — I am a woman of the north," Belva boasted, strutting about and swinging a cedar branch. Then she asked facetiously, "Does that give me all the privileges of an *homme du nord*?"

I thought it best not to answer, and turned to start over the portage. Feeling quite regal in our self-appointed roles of northmen, we walked up the path in solemn procession over a royal carpet of leaves.

"Look, this is part of the ridgepole of North America," Belva said, as she examined a sign, halfway over the portage. Obviously broken by a disgruntled bear, the sign read LAURENTIAN HIGHLAND DIVIDE.

The waters south and east of the divide flow to the Atlantic through the Lake Superior–St. Lawrence drainage system (which we had been traversing from Grand Portage to this point). The waters north of the divide flow to Hudson's Bay through the Rainy Lake drainage system (which we were now to follow as far as Rainy Lake). For the voyageurs the divide was merely the secondary reason for their ceremony, the primary one being an excuse to drink a little high wine.

Making merry must have been the order of the day on this portage, for as Henry the younger remarked: "At this place the men generally finish their small kegs of liquor and fight many a battle."

We continued on, making a reversed S curve through North Lake (Lac du Hauteur des Terres) at its lower end. We were fascinated by the lake's high hills on the east and by the turquoise water "so cleare as christial."

Coming to a narrow channel, we made Décharge des Epingles, now a portage because of low water. Two hundred feet long, it passes around a small pin-shaped rapid and follows a short section of an old railroad built to carry iron ore from Gunflint Lake to Fort William.

Soon we were paddling over the roughened surface of Gunflint Lake (Lac des Pierres à Fusil), about seven miles long and one to two miles wide, running in a west-southwesterly direction. Hills covered with aspen and birch and stands of pine and balsam surround the lake. The flint which abounds on its shores was used by the voyageurs in their flintlock guns.

"Do you suppose Rolf is here?" Belva asked, as we pulled up to the dock at Kerfoot's Lodge.

"I hope so," I answered. "It's a shame to miss the Granite River. Everyone has said it's so beautiful, but we'd better not tackle it in this low water."

This river took the voyageurs from Gunflint Lake, at its northwest corner, to Saganaga. It is a winding twelve-mile chain of small lakes separated by narrows which require frequent *décharges* and portages, the number depending on the water level.

The lateness of the season and recent scarcity of rain had made the water level low all along the border, but the Granite River was particularly low. Rolf Skrien, a canoe outfitter on Saganaga, had advised us that the twelve-mile Granite River was unnavigable in places, and that it would slow us up a day or more to attempt it. He had kindly offered to meet us at Gunflint Lake and drive us to Saganaga over the Gunflint Trail. We had reluctantly decided to omit that part of our trip.

Rolf did meet us, and took us over the Gunflint Trail so that we could bypass the river.

"Have a nice trip," Rolf said with a friendly grin as we paddled away from the dock at the end of the road. We went down the Sea Gull River to Saganaga, then to the mouth of the Granite River, before we resumed our journey.

Now we would follow the waters which flow north to Hudson Bay, through Saganaga, Basswood, and Lac la Croix. Formed differently from the eastern lakes, these lakes lie in solid rock basins, some of granite, as at Saganaga and Lac la Croix, and others are greenstone and slate.

At last we had reached the Quetico-Superior and were completely happy. This was our own canoe country, whimsical in mood, with wild and ever-changing beauty. Challenged by man, but left inviolate, it is a special place of vast and ancient peace. Here are lakes whose waters may lash with spuming fury at rocks and sandy beaches, or rest expansively in luminous tranquility. Here is an extravagance of bays and islands, each with secret places waiting to be found. On the shores are fissured cliffs, thick with clinging lichens, mosses, and ferns. There are hills with venerable forests of pine, and valleys crowded with fragrant balsam and cedar, flashed with white birch and maple. Rivers whip white through narrow gorges, then bend to flow quietly through lush marshlands hiding ducks and beavers and moose.

We paddled with renewed vigor down the little river, then followed the east shore of Saganaga almost to the mouth of the Granite River. Here we inspected a point of land, l'Anse de Sable, or Handle of Sand, which had long been the site of an Indian canoe factory. Henry the younger stopped here in 1800 and found "some Indians making canoes for sale; but as none of them were to my taste, we proceeded to the détroit in the lake."

From the Handle of Sand we went a short distance into Red Sucker Bay and passed Rocky Point. We would have stopped, if we had had time, for evidence has been found there of a Hudson's Bay post of which we could find no record in the journals.

Saganaga, the largest body of water we had encountered, is extremely irregular in outline. The Indian name it still retains was derived from the many islands of rock and pine which crowd the southeastern half of the lake. The course through it is twelve miles in a northeast–southwest direction.

We entered the island-cluttered lake cautiously, dodging from one island to another to stay in the lee of a strong northwest wind which rolled the water's surface into whitecaps and chased piles of clouds across the sky.

The sun highlighted the lichen-mantled cliffs and the plume-like branches of their overtowering white pines. Its light searched into the deep bays of the sprawling lake and revealed, through the haze, the purple hills behind them. Saganaga seemed far more primitive and wild than the other lakes we had traveled across.

We passed Voyageur Island, a favorite campground of the French-Canadian canoemen, and fought our way toward Red Rock Bay, then turned back up the lee shore of American Point. The breakers crashed and shattered against granite rocks piled on shore. We worked our way through the high waves, the prow of the canoe rising and falling with a rude smack on each one, and finally landed at dark, just short of the rocky point.

Unloading the canoe quickly so that the waves would not break it on the rocks, we climbed over more of the huge jagged rocks to look for a campsite.

"Damn!" exclaimed Belva, as she slipped in the dark and hit her knee solidly on the hard granite. "These may be the oldest granites in North America, but I *know* they're the hardest."

The flashlight, searching here and there, showed not a foot of ground free of rocks or trees. Since we had no choice, up went the tent — the left corner on top of a small spruce, a rock in the middle of the floor and the right front corner riding high on another. No tent ever stood at a more uncertain angle! There was at least one consolation: the rocks were padded with springy moss.

We were cold and uneasy in the wind. Stumbling around in the dark, we gathered pine cones and pieces of bark. Belva laid the tinder in a crevice and lit it. The fire wouldn't catch, so she knelt and blew gently on the smoldering sticks. Sparks cracked and spit and flew upward. They burst into flames, and then burned brightly as we added sticks of wood. Soon we were warmer, and water for our tea bubbled in the pot.

After supper we sat on rocks around the blazing fire, surrounded by ragged jackpines. Their branches were dead and snarled, and draped with old-man's-beard. The fire's light flickered through the tangle and caught in the festooned lichens. Beyond was the blackness of the forest. The wind rushed through the larger pines, tossing and swaying their protesting branches. It brought the waves crashing rhythmically against the rocks on shore.

In the east Mars shivered red and the Pleiades danced overhead, cold and distant. In the northern sky a curtain of ethereal light hung in trembling folds of white, blue, and green, fading and pulsing in ghostly configuration. Streamers of red surged up into the luminous veil of color. From the dark reaches over the lake came the excited honking of geese in flight. Truly, this was the north country in a savage mood.

We sat in companionable silence, growing drowsy as the fire died. Then we crawled into our warm sleeping bags.

As I lay listening to the fury that continued to rage outside, I remembered what Alexander Henry the elder had said of Saganaga in 1775. "This was the hithermost post in the northwest, established by the French; and there was formerly a large village of Chipeways here, now destroyed by the Nadowessies [Sioux]. I found only three lodges, filled with poor, dirty and almost naked inhabitants, of whom I bought fish and wild rice, which latter they had in great abundance. When populous, this village used to be troublesome to the traders, obstructing their voyages, and extorting liquor and other articles."

Though this was not the hithermost post of the French, I could see the French merchant here in those early days. Irving described him as "a kind of commercial patriarch. With the lax habits and easy familiarity of his race, he had a little world of self-indulgence and misrule around him. He had his clerks, canoe-men, and retainers of all kinds, who lived with him on terms of perfect sociability, always calling him by his Christian name; he had his harem of Indian beauties, and his troop of half-breed children; nor was there ever wanting a louting train of Indians, hanging about the establishment, eating and drinking at his expense in the intervals of their hunting expeditions."

In a sudden gust, the wind billowed the tent and tugged at its hasty moorings. But, already half asleep, I felt disinclined to worry, and only burrowed deeper into my sleeping bag.

October 7

LAKE SAGANAGA TO CYPRESS LAKE

W E AWOKE early. The wind had calmed overnight, and in the cold air our breath formed frosty vapor as we talked.

"How about a cup of hot coffee, please?" Belva shouted to Harvi, who had already built the fire. We could hear its crackling and smell its piney fragrance.

"All I can offer you is a kettle of iced tea," Harvi said, tying back the tent flap. "You'll have to wait a while for coffee."

Looking out, we saw what he meant. It had frozen overnight, and our leftover tea was solid in the kettle. A glaze of ice capped the rocks on the shore. Out on the lake islands huddled behind banks of silent fog that obscured the rising sun.

Reluctantly we left our sleeping bags, dressed in a hurry, and then went to warm our hands at the fire. After washing down our breakfast with several cups of scalding coffee, we broke camp. Loading the canoe was a perilous job. Slipping precariously on the steep icy rocks, we finally accomplished it, and shoved off into the wind toward the point.

"I don't know whether we can make it," Harvi said with a concerned look as we rounded the point. The wind was blowing full again, sweeping whitecaps across Cache Bay and dashing them against the shore we were about to follow.

We began taking in water as the waves almost engulfed us. "Let's get out of here!" Belva shivered in her drenched clothes. Harvi headed for shore.

"We are degraded!" I exclaimed, as the canoe ground into the sandy beach.

"I don't know about that, but we're sure as hell windbound," Harvi said with disgust.

A *dégradé*, in voyageur language, meant being forced by strong winds to land or to remain at an encampment. The voyageurs would offer La Vieille, the old woman of the wind, tokens of tobacco to calm her, so they could continue their journey.

The voyageurs and their passengers frequently suffered wettings in their voyages. Many times they were delayed for a day after a crossing in rough water, a *dégradé*, or an upset in a rapid. Fires were built to dry clothes and papers. Packs of trade goods and furs were opened and spread. Sheets and linens were draped on nearby trees and bushes. When all was dry, off they would go again.

Harvi had a driftwood fire going as fast as the voyageurs could have said "Jean Baptiste." We crowded around it to dry our clothes and warm ourselves, then spent the rest of the morning exploring the small beach and loafing in the sun behind a sheltering cliff.

During our leisurely lunch of flapjacks that oozed butter and syrup, a windblown chipmunk skittered down the cliff and joined us. He graciously accepted a syrupy morsel. Enthroning himself on a choice piece of firewood, he consumed every crumb, then imperiously demanded more. Afterwards he licked his paws and cleaned his whiskers, sputtering indignantly at the stickiness.

"Wish we could make the portage, but it doesn't look as though we will," Belva said. "So why don't you read what our companions had to say about Gunflint, the Granite River, and Saganaga?"

It seemed a good idea; so after another swallow of coffee, I opened my notes and read Bigsby first.

"We next passed into the West Lake of the Height of Land, by a carrying place (468 yards long) profusely loaded with trees, shrubs, and grass. We are now in waters tributary to Hudson's Bay, and seventy-eight miles from Lake Superior.

"The West Lake is five miles and a half long, but its principal part lies to the east of our route, and is surrounded by very high hills. We therefore cross it obliquely towards the north (one mile and a third), passing by porphyry of silicious base *in situ* on a point close to our route on the east.

"We now gain access to Gunflint Lake (six miles and a third by two miles) by two sets of narrows and rapids, altogether three miles long.

"Gunflint Lake often takes the name of Redground Lake, from the ochrey red gravel with which it abounds, and the ferruginous colour of its basalt. We find on it greenstone porphyry in lofty hills, with fine olivine or feldspar crystals; most likely a part of the basaltic and cupriferous rocks of Lake Superior.

"Leaving this lake we descended to the still larger lake, Keseganaga, by a series of five small basins (or lakes) and narrows; the whole twelve miles long, and often the seat of rough rapids, — the scenery of hills, shattered rocks, and turbulent waters being savage in the extreme, especially at the portage of the Wooden Horse.

"The moment we entered this chain of waters, the high table-lands, the cliffs, the rich vegetation of a basaltic district, the regular outlines of the lakes, the absence of islands, were exchanged for a naked country of granite, in mounds, either piled one upon another or single (low, perhaps), and surrounded by wide marshes; the prevailing tints of the country being red and dark grey; the former from the granite or gneiss, and the latter from the admixture of scorched pines and young poplars everywhere filling the eye.

"There are several very fine cascades in these twelve miles, almost rivalling the best in the Canadas. The occasional rapids were so strong and billowy as to shake the canoe severely.

"On the Height of Land one of our *voyageurs* was seized with inflammation of the bowels, which bleeding, &c. subdued only for a time, — being reproduced by the roughness of the waters. The man's agony and exhaustion were extreme. We were, therefore, exceedingly glad to see, on

88

"Lake Superior" by Frances Ann Hopkins

"Shooting the Rapids" by Frances Ann Hopkins

"Bivouac of Canoe Party" by Frances Ann Hopkins

"Canoe Party around a Campfire" by Frances Ann Hopkins

Upper Basswood Falls, an illustration from John Bigsby's *The Shoe and Canoe*, 1850

"Canoe Proceeding along High Rocky Cliffs" by Frances Ann Hopkins

Lac La Croix, an illustration from John Bigsby's
The Shoe and Canoe, 1850

Sir George Simpson, Hudson's Bay Company Governor,
on an inspection tour

entering Lake Keseganaga, a large wigwam, on a marshy point, belonging to a well-known old Indian named Frisée. He had two or three strong sons and three or four daughters and daughters-in-law, and their children, all looking brown and fat, although said to be starving.

"Frisée willingly received the sick man, but said that both hunting and fishing had failed them; that his young men had been out four days and had only killed two rabbits. The *voyageur*, he said, must be content with family fare. And on landing I was not a little disturbed by seeing two men and a woman, at the entrance of the wigwam, feeding with their fingers, out of a tub, on the unwashed entrails of a rabbit, and wiping their hands, when they had done, on their own heads or on the back of a dog.

"There was no help for it — stay our man must; so Mr. Astronomer Thompson prepaid Frisée one-half of the proposed reward in tobacco and coarse blue cloth, promising the remainder on our return to receive our man again. I gave some yards of tape and of scarlet and yellow riband to the girls, who are very fond of such things.

"To our friend we gave tobacco and biscuit. He was content to stay, and nodded languidly to his comrades as they stepped into the canoe. When we had begun to move through the water I looked back, and saw behind the wigwam the children with my riband, cut into short pieces, tied in their hair. They were scampering and screaming with joy like little furies. Indian children are treated with great indulgence.

"Lake Keseganaga, down which we are now moving, is much larger than any we have yet seen; and pass along its length (fourteen miles). It is very irregular in shape, and derives its name from being full of islands Its south shore displays three ranges of heights; — first, the green slopes at the water's edge; secondly, a thinly-wooded purplish-red ridge; and thirdly, behind it, a blue line of hills, still higher, and visible along all this side of the lake.

"Its outlet is a river of the same name, which flows into Hudson's Bay by Lake Sturgeon of the New Route.

"Here we saw two bears (where the Indians had seen none); one was sitting at gaze on a high rock. As soon as he perceived us, he wheeled about, and hurried into the interior.

"We met with the other on our return home. What I took to be an old

October 6 – 10

Lac des Mille Lacs

KAMINISTIKWIA ROUTE

French L.

Twin Falls P.

Tanner's Rapids

Maligne R.

Sturgeon L.

Hunters' Island

PAINTED ROCK

Bottle L.

Curtain Falls P.

Crooked L.

Bottle P.

Iron L.

PAINTED ROCK

Lower Falls P.

Wheel Barrow P.

Basswood L.

Horse P.

A.F. CO. POST

FRENCH POST

H. B. CO. POST

Birch L.

Prairie P.

Carp P.

Carp L.

Knife Portages

Knife L.

Little Knife P.

Cypress L.

Monument P.

Swamp L.

Swamp P.

L. Saganaga

FRENCH POST

Granite R.

Gunflint L.

Pine P.

Height of Land

GRAND PORTAGE ROUTE

hat floating in a wide expanse of water was declared to be a bear. Bears swim low. Both canoes made for him as fast as we could paddle, and we soon came up with poor Bruin.

"Our astronomer took his stand at the bow, and quietly discharged his piece into his neck. The animal gave a loud howl, and rolled about in the bloody water violently, while we struck at him with poles and an axe. So great was the hubbub that I thought we should all have been drowned, for a small birch canoe is the last place to make war in; but the bear being soon stunned and quiet, a *voyageur* laid hold of him by the neck, and we slowly drew him to the shore.

"When on dry land, and the water had ran off a little, the bear suddenly revived, stood up and showed fight, but he was so weakened by loss of blood that a few more blows on the head laid him low for ever. He was skinned that evening, and we made three good meals of him. Fresh meat is a luxury those only can estimate who have been living on salt provisions for some time in hot, steaming woods.

"We saw but few bears this summer, but in that of 1824 the party met with nearly twenty, owing probably to a new distribution of food making fruit or fish more plentiful here than elsewhere."

"Gee, we haven't seen hide nor hair of a bear so far," Belva complained.

"Don't be disappointed. You may come face to face with one yet," I answered, and handed her the notebook containing Delafield's description. "Here, it's your turn."

As I leaned back to listen I saw our lunchtime companion perched on a ledge bright-eyed and curious, as though listening intently.

"The lake on the W. side of the Height of Land also called A-ja-wa-wa Sagagan, or Height of Land Lake, is a pretty little lake, from which we pass by a narrow strait to Pin Portage. This is a short rapid about the length of the canoe and descent about three feet. We are nevertheless induced to carry the heavy baggage, and the canoe with a few light things saults the rapid, as is the phrase of the country. It is a narrow pass thro' angular green stone rocks thrown there by the force of currents and drawing to a point: the rapid takes a similar form, from which circumstance I presume the name. Chert or flinty substances associate with the green stone at Pin Portage, and blue calcedony in considerable quantities but not very fine . . . In the N.E. are to be seen some high bluffs or mountain ranges, but there is a change from the country the other side of the Height. After passing a narrow strait, with low flats on each side, that contracts to a pass filled with rushes, the Flint Lake, or Pierre au Feu Lac of the Canadians, suddenly displays a handsome shoot, or rather strait. It is 9 miles long and less than a mile wide. On the right of the entrance to the lake is a short and clean sand beach, a sight so novel was quite welcome after roving so many days on rocky shores that scarcely allowed a foot hold, or even approach. The Indian name of Flint Lake is Kam-squat-se-ka. It is surrounded by the green stone formation passing into slate, which is sometimes ferruginous, and contains flint, black and blue calcedony. Small fragments abound on the shores. Course of Flint Lake S.W. The ragged Highlands with perpendicular faces have disappeared, and ranges of hills with moderate inclinations supply their places. I know of no better mode of describing the direction of the Highlands in these regions, than to say that the water courses and lakes conform to them and are generally E. & W., but vary even to N. & S. If any general remarks can be made of the country thus far it is that N.E. and S.W. are the prevailing courses of the Highlands. We took a turtle of 6 or 7 lbs. weight in Flint Lake which was like the common fresh water turtle. Neither my inquiries or observation have led to the discovery that the web-footed turtle exists in these waters including the Great Lakes, some traveller to the contrary notwithstanding. A narrow strait carries us from Flint Lake, again swelling into a little lake one mile, to a short rapid of two feet fall which we descend with the aid of the canoe line. Close to this rapid is the l'Escalier Falls Portage. The l'Escalier Falls as the name indicates, is in steps, and the descent may be, together with the rapid, just above 18 feet. A reddish granite with green feldspar is the rock formation of this neighborhood.

". . . A portage of course is made here, and again embarking we shortly arrive at the Wooden Horse Rapid and Fall. The rapid we shoot with loaded canoe and, it being about sun set, encamp on the portage of the Wooden Horse Falls. This portage is over rocks, about one hundred yards in length. The falls are broken, or in several steps, and including the rapids above are about thirty feet fall. . . .

92

"Have remarked since leaving the Height of Land the old water level to be seen on the rocks, indicating that in former time it was much higher than at present. In some of the lakes it has been four feet above the present level, and from four feet it varies to one in different lakes, according to the outlet produced by the cause that effected the change. The waters at this time, are higher than they usually are. The change, however, is very sudden in the interior, depending upon the quantity of rain, and the same season shews both higher and lower waters than the voyageurs are accustomed to. As regards the ancient water levels, I have remarked them from the St. Lawrence River to this place, and can only say that I consider the decrease to be regular by the wearing away of the barriers; and the irregularity of the diminutions in different lakes may depend upon the rock formation of its outlet, it being evident that the lime stone, the slate and the granite would yield at different degrees of pressure.

"Sunday, July 20. The portage of the Wooden Horse Falls where I encamped last night is a rude and romantic spot. Pitched my Marquee on the only flat rock there was of sufficient size for it, in the middle of the portage by the side of the falls. The cascades are tumbling thro chasms of granite, and being in several shoots, in all 30 feet, the noise is very great. But these sounds are so familiar that I lose no rest & embark soon after sun-rise. Pass thro' a strait that leads to a portage of one post, called the Great Pine Portage, having breakfasted whilst the men were carrying on the portage and, the usual ceremony of gumming the canoe being performed, embark on the strait from Great Pine Portage and shortly arrive at Siskile Rapid. Sault this rapid which is thro walls of granite quite regularly shaped.

". . . Shortly after avoid another bad rapid by carrying heavy luggage over a portage and sault the canoe. Descent 6 feet. Soon descend another difficult rapid, and very soon after arrive at another, where we are again obliged to unload, and carry the heavy articles over a very bad portage, and sault the canoe. My guide calls it the Mariboo Rapid.

"Thence pass into Lake Saganaga which means Lake of Bays. This is a large lake, and contains, by Mr. Ferguson's surveys, two hundred and eighty-nine islands. In my passage thro' it I could form no idea of the size or direction of the lake, it was so glutted with islands, both large and small.

The maps sent me by Mr. Ferguson of his last year's work terminate here, and after advancing about 2 hours in groups of islands, my old guide acknowledges that he is lost, and we know not which way to proceed. A setting sun adds to the difficulty, but roving about the guide recognizes the track & we soon find an encamping ground that had apparently been the frequent resort of times past, and proved a comfortable lodgement. The rock formations have been granite with hornblende throughout the day's travelling."

Later that afternoon the wind died, so we paddled the remaining two and a half miles to the narrows of Saganaga.

Now our course would take us through the chain of lakes and portages which form the southeast boundary of Hunters' Island, called *Ile des Chasseurs* by the French, from the Indian name meaning hunter. It is an island only in that its land is completely surrounded by lakes and rivers, except for a small strap of land between Swamp and Cypress Lakes. After traversing its southeast boundary we would follow the southwest boundary, consisting of Basswood Lake, the Basswood River, Crooked Lake, and Lac la Croix. The island's northwest boundary is the Maligne River and Sturgeon Lake, while its northeast side consists of the Saganagons and Kawnippi chain through Cache Bay, near the narrows of Saganaga.

Threading our way through the narrows, we came to Swamp portage (Portage Rocher de la Prairie), a lift leading into Swamp Lake. We passed through this lake, a mile long and hemmed in by yellow tamaracks, to Monument Portage (Portage la Prairie), ninety-six rods long.

The portage starts at the east end, in a grassy spot surrounded by marsh, then rises steeply over a ridge and down to Cypress, or Ottertrack Lake. Three cement and metal monuments, one at either end and in the middle, mark the boundary along the trail.

I sat at the end of the portage contemplating my wearisome packs and looking at the steep climb ahead. I took heart when I thought of the load seventy-five voyageurs carried over here in 1775. They came in twelve canoes belonging to James McGill, Benjamin Frobisher, and Maurice Blondeau. Sweating and cussing, they struggled with 100 gallons of rum and brandy, 24 kegs of wine, 64 kegs of gunpowder, 90 bags of ball and shot, 150 rifles, 150 boxes of dry goods, 15 trunks of dry goods, 12 boxes

94

of ironware, 12 nests of brass kettles, 100 packages of carrot and twist tobacco, 50 kegs of hogs' lard and tallow, and 60 kegs of pork.

Reaching the top of the ridge through storms of autumn leaves, Harvi and I dropped our loads and sat down to rest.

"Sure have been following these things all the way," Harvi said, patting a boundary marker on which he leaned.

"Yes, and we'll keep on following them," I added.

"How come?"

"Because they mark the fur traders' 'customary' road, which we are following," I answered. "The treaty of 1783, following the American Revolution, stated that the boundary line from Lake Superior to Lake of the Woods was to follow the traders' 'customary' one. Then Britain and the United States hassled and wrangled for many years as to where this route was. Commissions were set up and surveys made. In fact that's what Bigsby and Delafield were here for. The British claimed the route ran up the St. Louis River and through Vermilion and Crane Lakes. This would have given them more territory."

"You mean I could be living in Canada, instead of the United States, if they had gotten their way?" interrupted Harvi.

"Yes," I answered. "We would have lost the Arrowhead and the Iron Range if they had. We can thank Delafield for our not losing them. To offset the British claim he asserted the Kaministikwia was the 'customary' way. This would give the United States more territory. Actually the route we have been following was the usual one of the traders. It had been used for seventy-three years, while the St. Louis River route was little used, and the Kaministikwia only some sixty years before 1821. Had Grand Portage not been on American soil it would have been used even longer. In fact, the voyageurs, according to David Thompson, had to be 'coaxed and bribed' into the use of the Kaministikwia route. Anyway, in 1842 it was finally settled. The Webster-Ashburton Treaty said the Grand Portage route was the 'customary' road, and so the boundary was determined. Incidentally, the treaty also said 'that all the water communications and all the usual portages along the line from Lake Superior to the Lake of the Woods, and also Grand Portage, from the shore of Lake Superior to the

Pigeon River, as now actually used, shall be free and open to the use of the citizens and subjects of both countries.' "

"You learn something every day." Harvi swung the canoe up to his shoulders and started down the hill.

We set off on Cypress Lake and, after passing a third of the way through, camped on a cypress-covered point. Our campsite, snug and secure, carpeted with soft reindeer moss and sheltered by cedars, was a perfect place for tired voyageurs. Harvi built a fire with dry peeled aspen poles which he had picked up from beaver lodges along the way. While he was cooking supper over its clean hot flames, a barred owl called in the distance, "Who cooks for you? Who cooks for you?"

"Harvi, of course, you silly bird," Belva answered. "And I'm going to eat it."

After we had eaten I sat contented, immersed in the quiet beauty before me. Across the mirror bay the pine-topped hills sloped gently down to the water. Between the hills' green crests, troughs of gold overflowed where autumn-tinted birch grew in the ravines. At the shore's edge smoothly rounded boulders rested, half in the reflecting surface of the lake. Billowing clouds rolled over the tops of the hills, glowing pearl-pink in the last warm rays of the sun. The whole was perfectly reflected in the water. Then, with whistling wings and soft articulations, two mallard drakes skimmed across the bay and into the shadows at the far side of the lake. I was bewitched, I was sleepy, I went to bed and listened to the slap of beaver tails across the bay.

October 8

CYPRESS LAKE TO BASSWOOD LAKE

THE sun broke through the pines over the ridge as we sat in the still cool air drinking our after-breakfast coffee. We listened to the sounds of morning and watched hypnotized the rising and falling of the lake's glassy surface, until the sun warmed our backs. Then we got into the canoe and floated off into the bright morning. As we emerged from a small opening, the breathtaking beauty of Cypress stopped us.

"Isn't it lovely," Belva sighed.

We looked down the narrow body of water, about four miles long. Much like a river, its shores, fringed with cedars, rise perpendicularly from the emerald lake two to three hundred feet. The faces of these cliffs, colored with shafts of red, black, and orange, are reflected in the shimmering depths below. From the dense, dark green jackpine ridges bridging the cliffs to the waxy green lace of the cedars along shore extends a virgin forest of white pines and deep green balsams, brightened by the

97

yellow-green leaves and the white trunks of birch. Such spectacular beauty we had rarely seen, even in the north country.

We paddled on quietly, drinking deeply of the intoxicating air. Drunk with the heady magic of pine and balsam resins, I conjured up a brigade of birch canoes manned by scarlet-capped voyageurs. Their red paddles dipped into the sparkling water, then flashed in the sunlight as they lifted them for the next quick stroke. Their songs broke the cathedral silence of the lake, echoing and re-echoing from the cliff faces as they passed.

Then Belva broke the spell. She pointed toward shore at the cedars whose glossy frond-like branches just missed the water. "They look like fastidious ladies bending over to catch their reflections in the lake, and holding up their lace skirts so as not to wet them."

Soon we made Little Knife portage (Portage Petit Rocher des Couteaux) and lifted over the rock ridge beside a small cascade. We continued through Little Knife Lake until, passing through a narrow rockbound pass, we emerged into Knife Lake (Lac des Couteaux). It is about seven miles long and is named for the sharp pieces of slate which extend along its shores and fill its portage paths.

Knife was in a carnival mood. The wind was now out of the northeast, pushing huge rollers down the long unbroken stretch. We caught the lake's mood and rode the waves full speed past its mountainous shores. The shadows of clouds overhead sped along with us. Carried on by the wind, the prow of the canoe breaking through the glassy green rollers, we felt exhilarated, as though riding a roller coaster. Intoxicated with reckless abandon, we shouted heedlessly into the wind. Then a bald eagle, soaring with set pinions, suddenly dipped to water level just ahead, as if he were joining the party. For a few exciting moments he led us, but doubtless thinking us mad, he veered upwards and soared so high he became a mere speck.

We made Big Knife portage, forty-three rods, and continued on through small portages and *décharges* in the Knife River, through the three Petit Rocher des Couteaux portages. No name has ever been more appropriate, for the slates on the paths all lie with their knife-sharp edges exposed. It must have been sheer hell for the moccasined voyageurs. As for me, I wished I could have sheathed every one. We passed through the lower end

98

of Carp Lake and over Portage la Carpe, where Macdonell in 1793 mixed nine gallons of rum to "wet the whistle" of every Indian he met on the way. Crossing the four-mile length of golden Birch Lake we came to Prairie portage (Portage Gros des Bois Blanc), David Thompson's Great Whitewood Carrying Place.

The portage, 660 feet long on the American side, curves around a channel cut through steep banks. The water divides and then falls in a series of cascades as two streams into Basswood Lake (Lac Bois Blanc). As I crossed I wondered where, in August, 1797, David Thompson had "Found — 4 Sotees [Sauteur or Chippewa] & their families with about the Meat of 2 Moose dried — The House [bark hut] burnt to the Ground — About ½ PM the Rain became heavy & we put up — About 2 PM the Gentlemen [bourgeois] came & put up with us."

Looking out into Inlet Bay I recalled Mackenzie's remarks about the lake whose name he thought "improperly so called, as the natives name it the Lake Pascau Minac Sagaigan, or Dry Berries [blueberries]." He went on to describe its former inhabitants.

"Before the small pox ravaged this country [shortly after the conquest of Canada], and completed, what the Nadowasis [Sioux], in their warfare, had gone far to accomplish, the destruction of its inhabitants, the population was very numerous: this was also a favorite part, where they made their canoes, &c. the lake abounding in fish, the country round it being plentifully supplied with various kinds of game, and the rocky ridges, that form the boundaries of the water, covered with a variety of berries.

"When the French were in possession of this country, they had several trading establishments on the islands and banks of this lake. Since that period, the few people remaining, who were of the Algonquin nation, could hardly find subsistence; game having become so scarce, that they depended principally for food upon fish, and wild rice which grows spontaneously in these parts."

We set out on the voyageurs' course through Basswood, fifteen miles in the shape of a Z. We followed David Thompson's "Co. [Course] N20W ¾ mi. N60W 1/20 mi." through Inlet Bay. The wind had switched again As we left Inlet Bay we met row upon row of menacing whitecaps advancing at us from the west and threatening to engulf us.

"Look," Belva shouted, spotting a cape. "I'll bet that's where Bigsby and Delafield saw a Hudson's Bay post. Let's go look."

Almost upsetting in the attempt, we turned back and landed to explore the point. Starting at the edge of the timber, we worked our way across it through a brushy growth of alder, aspen, and maple.

"Here it is!" Belva exclaimed as she stood on a slight rise in the ground.

After following the outlines through the brush, she wiped the sweat from her forehead and said, "This *has* to be it. There seem to have been two buildings here."

"It is," I assured her. "Pieces of old English china, large fishhooks, square-headed nails and other evidence relating it to the Hudson's Bay Company have been found here."

"Sure doesn't seem to have been very big," Harvi said as he surveyed the area.

"It wasn't," I explained. "This post and all the others in the Quetico-Superior were merely small wintering houses. Each was subsidiary to the chief post of its company in this Lac la Pluie, or Rainy Lake, district. The larger forts were built near the falls on Rainy River."

Life went on in these houses during the frozen months much as it did at other wintering posts, large or small, throughout the Northwest. The only differences between the large and small ones were in the more extensive social life and the greater amount of work necessary in maintaining a larger establishment. Every year, in late summer, the traders and the voyageurs returned to their wintering places in canoes loaded with trade goods. Depending on the period, the Nor'Westers came from their summer Rendezvous at Grand Portage, or later Fort William. The Hudson's Bay men came from Fort Garry, and the American Fur traders from Fond du Lac on the St. Louis River.

Once settled they busied themselves with preparations for the long winter. Repairs to buildings were made: fresh cedar bark replaced broken bark on roofs, white clay plaster chinked cracks in the logs of the shop, a new floor was laid in the men's house. Nets were set at the mouths of rivers and others mended for later use. Sacks of wild rice were bought from the Indians who had just harvested the "water oats" that grows in such profusion in the border lakes. Kegs of maple sugar, obtained the pre-

100

ceding spring from squaws, were brought out and checked. Indian hunters were hired to augment the supply of fresh meat through the winter. Wood was cut and piled high.

As the snows descended and the lakes froze, life settled into a daily routine. Indian customers, rival traders, men from other posts — all filled the days with their comings and goings. Frequent trips were made throughout the winter to Indian camps for furs and food, and to other posts with supplies and letters. Early in the subzero mornings dogs were wrestled into tandem harnesses and hitched four in a train to toboggan-shaped sleds, or *traineaux de glace*. The dogs in their bells, gaudy robes, and leather boots howled and frisked about, eager to start the trip, or *dérouine*. Then, to a cry of Marche! and the crack of a whip, off they went, pulling their five-hundred-pound loads over the snowy trails. Only the yelping of the dogs and the shouting of the voyageurs — "*mouche*" (increase speed), "*y'ui*" (turn right), and "*sacre chien mort*" (damned dead dog) — disturbed the frosty vacant silence. Riding and running, the voyageurs would drive up to sixty miles a day, stopping only every five miles for a pipe. At sunset, in a sheltered place, camp and supper were made. Later the men would lie down, feet to the fire, on beds of furs and blankets spread on balsam boughs. So they passed the night, getting up several times to refuel the fire. In the morning they were on the way again to complete their missions.

While some voyageurs were on *dérouine*, the resident bourgeois or clerk kept those at the fort busy. They cleaned the fort of snow, cut timber, made snowshoes, traps, and sleds, visited traplines, pulled fishnets placed under the ice, hunted for food, spied on rival traders, and intercepted Indians to prevent rivals from getting the furs. The clerks were engaged with blanketed Indians who came to trade their furs for guns, kettles, beads, or liquor. The women, halfbreed or Indian consorts of the men, were occupied with their many domestic activities.

Random passages from the diary of Hugh Faries, a clerk at the North West Company's Lac la Pluie post during the 1804–1805 season, give an idea of the daily round of activities. "Chenettes Girl was bro^t to bed of a daughter . . . La Verdure being unwell I gave him a vomit . . . Old Azure and his wife had a battle. he gave her a black eye. . . . Richard got ready with 4 Men to go to the indians . . . the men were employed making a chimney . . . the rest of the men plaistered their houses &c. . . . Richard brought a parcel of dried Meat, today, and the Indians had not yet made any Oats. . . . I was busy since yesterday making a Seine. . . . Richard & I set off to go a hunting in the lake [Rainy Lake], & met, the men returning from the Chaudiere [Kettle Falls] with 10 50 White fish. . . . The men chopping fire Wood. . . . About 12 oclock I sent M^r McCrae, with men off to winter at the Dalles, along side of the X.Y. . . . The Seiners came home with 50 Sturgeons. . . . Got some logs squared today for the new house. . . . Old Godin got wood home to make 2 traines. . . . I was inform'd by Laverdure, that the X.Y. were preparing to go a *deroûine*. Accordingly I got Goods &c. ready to follow them & kept three men all night about their fort watching them. . . . In the evening La France return'd without finding the indians. . . . I got the snow thrown out of the fort. . . . The women netted 3 p^rs Snow Shoes. . . . In the evening, arrived one of the Pines. he was obliged to eat the few Skins he killed. . . . I sent 4 men off to the *Pêche d' hiver* [winter fishing grounds], with Nets, to fish. . . . Some of the men visiting and making traps. . . . Kashishwa came down for the payment of his Skins. I paid him & he took for 20 plus [equivalent in furs of 20 large beaver blankets] on credit. . . . I sent La Verdue with 2 others to Lac Plat, with a few Goods & letters to M^r McIntosh & M^r McCrae. . . . We saw Bustards today for the first time. . . . The old Toad arrived with one of his Sons, they bro^t 50 plus. . . . Mr Grant's Girl traded about 30 ^lbs Sugar [maple sugar] today for Rum. . . . Richard with 3 men and one of Mr Lacombe's men, set off very early for the Meccane [Namakan Lake], to endeavor to draw in my debts &c. with the indians of that place. . . . In the evening, arrived the Devil with only 2 dress'd skins. . . . I got 23 Packs press'd today. . . . In the evening Mr Grant arrived from Vermillion Lake [probably the post at the mouth of Vermilion River], with 16 Packs of 96 ^lb each. . . . The Big Rat's son arrived, he brought only 1 dress'd Skin."

But life was not all work at the wintering posts. On holidays the men were free to celebrate, and celebrate they did. New Year's Day started with a visit to the house of the bourgeois or clerk to exchange embraces for a treat of high wine. The remainder of the day was spent drinking, feasting, fighting, and dancing. Ordinarily, at the end of a normal day's routine, after supper, the voyageurs would gather in front of the clay fireplace, smoking and talking (except on Sunday, which was reserved for dancing). Invariably someone would take down a fiddle and begin to play. The others would start singing to its accompaniment, and soon their songs would penetrate the walls of the small log house to join those of the wind in the snowy pines.

"Let's get started," Harvi said impatiently. "This wind is going to get stronger."

We battled the waves past Bayley Bay and Norway Point. Maneuvering out of the wind into a group of islands, we landed on the north side of one of those adjacent to Ottawa Island. It was 6 P.M. and dark. Again our campsite was a rock pile, but fortunately this time the rocks were flat. The tall Norways and old cedars around us looked friendly, especially when the yellow light from Harvi's fire washed their green needles and fan-like sprays with gold.

We felt, after supper, as Radisson and Groseilliers had: "There belly full, there mind without care, wearyed to the utmost of the foremost day's journey, fell a sleepe securely."

"That's what I'd like to do." Belva said with heavy eyes.

"No, don't go to sleep," I pleaded. "We can't neglect our companions tonight."

So I read Bigsby from the notebook.

"Leaving Lake Keseganaga, we again found ourselves among basaltic hills and marshes; and after a couple of carrying-places, passing down Cypress Lake (five ? miles long), and its near neighbour, Knife Lake (nine miles and a half long).

"The soil of these portages is two-thirds primitive gravel, the rest sand and brown clay.

"On Knife Lake I saw a cypress whose bark had been stripped by lightning from top to bottom, in a spiral three inches broad. I have seen other trees so treated.

"A succession of rapids, closely shrouded in foliage, sometimes violent (and an expanse, sometimes called Carp Lake), bring us into Boisblanc

103

Lake (fifteen miles long — Mackenzie), so called from its producing basswood.

"Its many islands, high and well-wooded shores, with pretty beaches of yellow sand, render it very picturesque. We passed a wintering-post of the Hudson's Bay Company, consisting of two or three comfortable huts on a cape.

"Boisblanc Lake is very crooked, and resembles the letter Z in shape. I found here the *Etheria exitiosa*, the destroyer of peach trees, as determined by Say of Philadelphia; but I saw no peach-trees.

"On our return home in autumn through this lake we espied a canoe rounding a point to enter one of its deep bays. Being then very short of provisions we hastened after it, and found it in company with four others, all filled with Indians. They could only sell us some strips of dried deer's flesh, each a yard long and four or five inches broad. It looked like thick, red leather; but our men were glad of it to thicken their soup. While this purchase was going on, the gentle breeze drove a canoe full of women alongside of mine. As we rocked on the wave, the women fixed their eyes with wonderment upon me sewing on a button. The needle having an eye, and carrying the thread along with it, caused many a low, soft note of surprise; but when I presented a needle and some thread to each of the dark ladies, they were delighted. Although their prattle was unintelligible to me, not so their thankful eyes."

"Belva, you're nodding," I said. "Delafield's long tonight, but keep awake. This is good."

"Monday, July 21. Embark at sun rise. . . . Clear.

"Leave Lake Saganaga over a short portage called the Little Rock Portage of Lake Saganaga. It is the length of the canoe only. There is here a little brook rippling over cobble-stones about a yard wide and three or four inches deep, thro' which the water runs into Lake Saganaga. It is covered with bushes, and without some examination would not be noticed. The Line of course will deviate once more from the old canoe route at this lake, and instead of pursuing it will follow the water communication which is by the River Saganaga as the Indians call it. This river is some distance N. of this little portage. Is said to be a large river with many bad rapids, and to connect by small lakes, with the Sturgeon Lake on the New

104

Road; and thence by the River Malin with Lake St. Croix & thence on-
ward by the Old Road. This deviation leaves on the S. of the Line & within
the U. S. Knife Stone Lake, Bois Blanc Lake, & Crooked Lake with the
connecting waters. In the Bois Blanc Lac is a British trading post (wintering house from fort at l'Pluie).

"Having no knowledge at this time of the above deviation but from
account obtained thro' Mr. Ferguson, & my guide being altogether ignorant
of it, I continue by the Old Road of the traders. Passing from Lake Saganaga, proceed over a small lake, called Lake l'Prairie to Portage l'Prairie
which take their name from a little marsh at the E. end of the portage. The
portage itself is rocky, and the compact green stone again occurs rising
about 20 ft. on the portage track. The rock of the little portage from Lac
Saganaga is granite. From Portage l'Prairie pass thro' a long, narrow and
circuitous strait, having on either side high cliffs of columnar green stone.
Its waters are deep. . . . It leads to the Knife Stone Lake Portage, so
called because of the angular fragments of green stone slate containing
flint, that abound here. It is a portage of about 150 feet, and the water
communicates over a fall of about 6 feet, running W. again. Knife Stone
Lake (or rather lakes because there are two, in fact, connected by a very
narrow pass obstructed with rocks thro which is a current), have high
cliffs on their sides (no doubt green stone); are long, narrow and winding,
having a general course W.S.W. The rock at the portage is a very compact
green stone, containing some iron and considerable white quartz.

"Knife Stone Lake leads to the Cedar Rapids which are six in number,
and we found them very bad and difficult to pass. Obstructed by fallen
trees that formed bridges over the passes, with a heavy growth of cedars
on the banks that gave a dismal darkness to them, together with roar of
rapids and the presence of rocks over which they dash'd, it was sufficiently
rude, without the fatigues that follow'd in descending them, to make the
scene sufficiently novel. The canoe was taken down with the load, the men
wading by its side to guide her safely by the rocks whilst I for part of the
distance scrambled thro the woods. When the water is higher, the descent
is said to be easy. When it is lower I am sure it must be difficult. Indeed,
a portage track in the woods was proof of this fact. Found some shells in
these rapids, and took specimens of the rock formation, which is a green

stone passing into slate. Pass the rapids and arrive at a fall, also known as the Cedar Fall & Portage and it being sun set, encamp.

"Night very warm, so much so that the blanket might for a time have been dispensed with, were it not for that most troublesome and most constant compagnon du voyage, the musquitoe. . . .

"Tuesday, July 22. Embark at sun rise from the first Cedar Portage and in ten minutes debark at the second. . . . The second Cedar Portage is also a short one. There are six rapids, and two portages, called the Cedar Rapids and Portages. The descent of the whole is about 40 feet. The next portage called by my guide the Sucker Portage, leads to a small lake of same name, and thence to Great Bois Blanc Portage. The Cedar Rapids and Portage to this place are all of green stone, running into slate. At the Bois Blanc Portage the green stone occurs in junction with granite. Descent of the falls at Bois Blanc Portage is about 15 feet. At this portage a small band of Indians and squaws perceiving us from their neighboring lodge came to us. Embark as soon as possible, to avoid both their thieving and begging. Give them some tobacco and leave them. When off they hailed to know if I would trade rum for skins & seemed surprised when told I had nothing to do with skins. When a mile from the portage, discovered that I had left my thermometer behind me & had little hope of recovering it, supposing the Indians had found it suspended in the bush. Returned and to my astonishment they had not perceived it.

"There is a wintering post for a trader of the Hudson's Bay Co. near the portage on the N. shore of this lake, that seems as if lately created. Mr. McGillivray from the Fort on River l'Pluie wintered here last year. It was deserted, but the wood pile indicated a return in the Winter. Lac Bois Blanc is called 18 m. long. It is filled with islands, and when in the middle of it my guide discovers that he is off the road, as the language of the country is, and we row about til near sun set from island to island before he is set right. Encountered several showers in the course of the afternoon & encamp on a sand beach skirted by the woods, from necessity."

Belva disappeared sleepily into the tent, while Harvi and I went to pull the canoe higher on shore. We stood there for awhile in the darkness, watching meteors like giant fireflies skidding through the sky in bright parabolas.

106

October 9. BASSWOOD LAKE TO CROOKED LAKE

Huge and red the sun rose. The morning mists and somber pines burst into flames as the fiery rays touched them. It seemed strangely eerie, resembling a circle in Dante's Inferno, especially when two horned grebes swam out of the mists like two little imps, to splash and preen near shore. Soon rising higher, the sun lost its redness and with an ethereal light made the wilderness again a paradise.

We broke camp and set out past Point au Pins, Point of Pines or Canadian Point.

"I'll bet it was over there." Belva pointed to Ottawa Island.

"No," I countered. "I think it was over there." I motioned toward another group of islands.

We were referring to Alexander Henry the younger's Pine Islands. He proceeded to these islands in 1800, after crossing Prairie portage and meeting three canoes from Rainy Lake loaded with Athabaska furs. There he "found a few Indians making canoes. Mine was in such a bad state that I could proceed no further; I therefore determined to wait for a new one

107

here, there being several on the stocks. The Indians were drinking and rather troublesome.

"Sunday, July 27. This morning we had rain, which continued until ten o'clock, when the weather cleared up, and the Indians set to work finishing my canoe. At eleven o'clock, four more canoes from Rainy Lake, with Athabasca packs, passed, and at one o'clock Roderick McKenzie [a Nor'-Wester] arrived in a light canoe [an express canoe without freight and manned by a picked crew], two days from Lac la Pluie, expecting to reach Grand Portage early on the 29th; he left at two o'clock."

"That's some real paddling," Harvi broke in.

I continued: "Several canoes overtook and passed me while I was impatiently waiting; but the Indians, from yesterday's debauch, were not in a working humor, and were continually smoking and begging for liquor. The weather was warm and sultry, which so increased their laziness that they finally fell asleep. The women brought me plenty of fine large hurtle-berries [blueberries here], of which there is an abundance on the rocks around this lake. Toward evening the Indians awoke and insisted upon my giving them liquor, otherwise I should have no canoe; and they threatened to break my old one. However, I persisted in refusing. We came to high words, and, in our turn, menaced them with a good beating if they misbehaved. This had the desired effect, and about midnight we got rid of them.

"July 28th. This morning the scoundrels refused to work, and I was obliged to set my own men to finish the canoe. She was completed at ten o'clock, when we loaded and embarked, giving the fellows a receipt for the canoe — 60 skins, payable at Lac la Pluie."

"Aluminum canoes are much more practical," Harvi said, patting the side of our canoe.

We crossed the open stretch and headed for U.S. Point. I looked south to Hoist Bay where, according to legend, an American Fur Company post may have been. A trade route led through the bay to Fall, Shagawa, Burnt-side, and Vermilion Lakes, and the Fond du Lac post near the mouth of St. Louis River. I turned toward the flats on U.S. Point, where the original Chippewa village had stood. The Indians had burned the point often to get a better crop of blueberries.

108

"Why do you suppose the voyageurs called this lake Bois Blanc?" Belva asked, as she looked around its shores. "If they named it for its basswood trees, there must have been more then than now."

"I don't think so," I answered. "The forests haven't changed that much."

"*Bois blanc* must have meant something other than basswood then," she reasoned, "because the voyageurs named lakes and portages for some feature easily recognized by everyone, not for an inconspicuous one."

I agreed.

"It couldn't have any connection with the Indian name either," she continued.

"Hardly; *Bashe-Meenong Saga-ai-gon* means Blueberry Lake."

Harvi had been taking it all in. "Don't suppose they meant cedar, do you?" He tipped his head toward the gentle shores, thick with pines and cedars. "Sure are lots of them. Maybe more then."

"I think you're on the track, Harvi," I said. "The traders even called U.S. Point Cypress Point because of its cedars."

"That makes sense," Belva said with assurance. "I'll bet the voyageurs meant the northern white cedar."

"I think that's right, Belva," I said. "You remember what Kohl says in *Kitchi Gammi* about the Indians using the bast of the cedar trees in making their canoes. And he says specifically that the voyageurs called the cedar *bois blanc*."

"Maybe some early traveler heard the voyageurs call the lake Bois Blanc and thought they meant Basswood, because that's what it means in French," Belva continued. "Or someone heard that the voyageurs got their *bast* wood here from all the cedars."

"Take your choice then: White Wood, Cedar, Blueberry, or Basswood," I concluded. "Maybe we'll never know."

We proceeded southwest, finishing the upper arm of the Z, to Upper Basswood Falls and the beginning of Basswood River.

Horse Portage starts just above the falls, and continues for a mile and a half through the woods, bypassing a series of rapids and cataracts that form a horseshoe curve in the river. It replaces two shorter portages which the fur traders used. They first made Little Basswood (Petit des Bois

Blanc), 140 yards around the falls, proceeded one and one half miles down river to Great Pine portage (Portage des Grand Pins), 330 yards around rapids, and continued down the river.

We walked a short way over Horse portage on a mosaic of crisp red and gold leaves, then put down our packs and went to look at the falls.

"It looks exactly as Bigsby drew it in 1823, even to the log," Belva commented. "All that's missing is the Indian with his poised spear, fishing."

The falls is a series of thundering cataracts in which the green water from Basswood pours over huge outcrops of granite, ribboned with white and rose quartz.

When we left the falls chickadees exploded out of the pines every few feet and accompanied us over the trail. We were on the down slope of a long hill of granite and had reached a level place where a quiet brook lazed across the path. Moss-covered stones offered precarious steps to the other side. Here was a natural place for a *posé*. Resting on silvery cushions of reindeer moss where the woods infringed on the rock, I admired the beauty of the forest floor. Had any of the voyageurs ever noticed it? I wondered. Surely their *chansons* tell us of their awareness of beauty.

So many shades and tints. Near the edge of the stream lay an olive-green sponge of sphagnum moss, and another kind, in reach of my hand, grew in a round kelly-green pillow of plush, buttoned in the center with a bright orange mushroom. Here was linnea, growing a garland around a pine knot. Next to it the waxy brightness of wintergreen and the heavy-veined star of bunchberry complemented each other. On a moldering stick grew a furry brown lichen edged in mauve, and some small cream and lavender fungi that spread like turkey tails.

I was examining a tuft of crimson-capped lichen trumpets when an acorn hit my hand. I looked accusingly at Belva, who merely laughed and glanced upward. A jay! Peck's bad boy in blue. He ruffed menacingly, shook his crest straight, and peered down. "Beat it, beat it!" he screamed.

"Come on," said Belva. "Let's humor him. It's time to go anyway."

He wasn't fooled by our nonchalant leavetaking. His jeers, loud and derisive, told us precisely what he thought. Only cowards would pick up and leave with so little provocation.

110

"Belva must be lost," Harvi said as he loaded the canoe at the end of the portage.

"No, she isn't," I replied. "As usual, she's picking up rocks."

"Again? What's she doing with them all?"

"You'd be surprised," Belva said as she arrived unnoticed.

We proceeded down the river, made a short portage around a shallow ripple, and came to Wheelbarrow Falls. Here there is a portage of fifty-six rods on the right — Portage de la Pointe Bois or Point of Woods portage.

We had rounded an island, midstream above the falls, and were headed for the portage when a merganser took off. The pattering of his red webbed feet, as he began his run, disturbed the black slick near the brink of the cascade. As he passed us we could see, only for a moment, his iridescent green head, narrow red bill, and white underparts. Soon his flight began, strong and direct, over the falls. Leaving the white churning water behind, he continued down river and into the sun.

We had made the portage and were starting downstream again when Belva grumbled, "I'm disappointed. I thought this river was supposed to be so rushing and dangerous. That's what some of the diarists wrote."

"Nothing to it now," Harvi said, "but in high water you wouldn't be disappointed."

"I wonder if the voyageurs had any wooden crosses here," Belva went on, half to herself. The voyageurs always erected simple wooden crosses on shore beside a rapids or falls where others had drowned. On passing these memorials, they would remove their red caps, cross themselves, and say a prayer to their patron saint.

All the way down the river we looked for Bigsby's pile of stones, a relic of ancient Indian warfare, but finding none, concluded it must be at Great Pine portage, which we had missed.

Finally we came to Lower Basswood Falls. Here the water shoots in two inclines around a central island and drops twelve feet into Crooked Lake. Its modern portage is on the right, thirty-two rods over a rock ridge. The portage in voyageur days, Petit Rocher du Lac Croche (Little Stone portage of Crooked Lake) was on the other side of the stream, where the absence of rocks on the river bottom meant safer landings for fragile canoes.

111

At this portage, as at all the others, the steersman and bowsman would spring into the water to keep the canoe from striking bottom or from grinding on shore. As the two men steadied the craft, the other voyageurs would jump out and unload the canoe. Hoisting their packs, they would start across the portage at a trot, with water dripping down their legs as they went. The canoe emptied, the steersman and bowsman would lift it out of the water and carry it upright across the portage, where the procedure was reversed. The canoe loaded, off the voyageurs would go down Crooked Lake, singing lustily.

It was noon, so we had lunch on a large flat rock beside the falls. Our flat rock reminded me of Garry's at Slave Falls, where the beauty of the place compelled him to open his locked brown leather diary and write, "Our Dinner Table was a hard Rock, no Table Cloth could be cleaner and the surrounding Plants and beautiful Flowers sweetening the Board. Before us the Waterfall, wild romantic, bold. The River Winnipic here impeded by Mountainous Rocks appears to have found a Passage through the Rocks and these, as if still disputing the Power of Water, show their Heads, adding to the rude Wildness of the Scene, producing Whirlpools, Foam loud Noise and chrystal Whiteness beautifully contrasted with the Black Pine. . . . The Wildness of the Scene was added to by the melancholy white headed Eagle hovering over our Board."

As I leaned against a tree to relax after lunch, I felt as happy as he had when "At the Foot of this magnificent Fall we dined . . . Indeed to my Feelings there is something very animating and inspiring in the Life of a Voyageur. In Nature's Wilds all is Independance, all your Luxuries and Comforts are within yourself and all that is pleasurable within your Minds; and after all this is Happiness, if there is such a thing in the World, which no Mortal can say. Indeed there is no Reasoning on Happiness."

There Garry's philosophizing stopped, and so did mine.

Nicholas Garry, the youthful bachelor deputy governor of the Hudson's Bay Company, was given the ticklish diplomatic task of bringing the proud Nor'Westers into the fold of the Hudson's Bay Company after union of the two companies in 1821. Confident of his ability, though he had little knowledge of the fur trade, this lonely Englishman left Montreal on June 13, 1821, with his servant, Raven, the two North West Company McGil-

112

livrays, a guide, and voyageurs. He followed the Nor'Westers' route over the Kaministikwia from Fort William as far west as the Red River, and then turned north to Hudson's Bay. The careful diary he kept is delightful reading and affords an intimate view of the fur trade. Garry accomplished his mission — the two companies were united. Then, unopposed, the Hudson's Bay Company could become the great corporation it is today.

After lunch we started through Crooked Lake (Lac Croche). Correctly named, it is divided into two parts: the first winds in a northerly direction, much like a river; the second passes in a westerly direction through a wider section with deep intricate bays, jutting rocky points, and enchanted islands.

Three miles from Lower Basswood Falls we came to David Thompson's "Arrows stick^g in a Rock." Here, on the face of a cliff which rises a hundred feet from the water, is a block of granite which formerly had a horizontal fissure. Recently the lower portion loosened and fell into the water below. Into the crack the Indians had shot numerous arrows whose bright-feathered shafts drew the attention of many early travelers.

"Look at the cliff," Belva said. "From the way it is colored, it looks as though some ancient abstractionist — a muralist no less — must have stood at the top and let his paints dribble over the edge. See: orange, black, gray, blue, and green. It looks as if the paint is still wet and trickling down into the lake."

The streaks of color extending down the face of the cliff were reflected in the oily smooth swells as they moved sinuously along the rock wall. It did indeed look as if the colors were running off the cliff and floating away in the water.

As our canoe slowly glided into the undulating bands of color, Belva was still admiring the granite wall. "I'd like to hear what our companions had to say about it."

"All right," I answered. "It's cool here in the shade and we need a rest anyway. Let's start with Mackenzie."

"Within three miles of the last Portage [Lower Basswood Falls] is a remarkable rock, with a smooth face, but split and cracked in different parts, which hang over the water. Into one of its horizontal chasms a great number of arrows have been shot, which is said to have been done by a war party of the Nadowasis or Sieux, who had done much mischief in this country, and left these weapons as a warning to the Chebois or natives [Chippewas], that, notwithstanding its lakes, rivers, and rocks, it was not inaccessible to their enemies."

"They must have had pretty good aim to put the arrows up there," Harvi said, as he looked toward the place where the crack had been.

Next I read David Thompson, who wrote in 1797: "in the crevices of a steep rock, about twenty feet above the water of a small lake [Crooked] are a number of Arrows which the Sieux shot from their Bows; the Arrows are small and short. The Chippaways, the Natives say: these Arrows are the voice of the Sieux and tell us, 'We have come to war on you, and not finding you, we leave these in the rocks in your country, with which we hoped to have pierced your bodies.' This was about the year 1730."

"I'll bet this was the same party of Sioux who killed La Vérendrye's son in Lake of the Woods," Belva said as I finished reading. She was referring to the massacre that took place on an island in Lake of the Woods in 1736. A party of Sioux warriors killed La Vérendrye's son, Jean Baptiste, and Father Aulneau, along with eighteen voyageurs. The group was on its way from Fort St. Charles to Grand Portage, to speed the arrival of the year's late provisions and trade goods. They were surprised by the Sioux, decapitated, and their heads wrapped in beaver skins.

Dr. Bigsby had this to say: "This narrow [of Crooked Lake] is walled in by high precipices of shattered granite, beautifully striped downwards by broad bands of white, yellow, red, green, and black stains (vegetable). Until lately, the arrows shot by the Sioux . . . might be seen, sticking in the clefts of the rocks."

In the same year, 1823, Delafield, who apparently had better vision through his metal-rimmed spectacles, wrote a more detailed description.

"A narrow strait with high granitic ridges on the sides and of deep water leads us to the Crooked Lake. In this strait, and on the left side just before emerging into the lake is a high perpendicular granite cliff rendered famous by the circumstance of its having in a fissure of the rock between 20 & 30 feet from the water a number of arrows, said to have been shot there by a war party of the Sioux when on an excursion against the Sauters or Chippewas. The party had advanced thus far and, not finding an enemy, shot

114

their arrows in the fissure as well to shew that they had been there, as to convince them of their deadly aim. The fissure presents an opening of two inches, and there may be seen still the feather ends of about twenty arrows driven nearly to the end."

"Wait, Harvi," I said. Thinking we had finished reading, he had started to paddle off. "Delafield tells of something the others hadn't mentioned."

"What's that?" he asked, putting his paddle down.

"He examined the cliff more thoroughly," I answered. "He 'Took a fragment of the rock, as somebody, I noticed, had done before me. The traveller has left his mark on this rock in various ways; some by name & some by date & some by strange device.'"

The "strange device" he referred to was, of course, the Indian pictographs. These drawings may be found today throughout the Quetico-Superior on the sheer faces of rock cliffs. They are painted as high as a man could reach standing in a canoe. Drawn on the rocks by primitive artists, with iron oxide and sturgeon oil as a binder, the reddish-brown pictographs — moose, hands, pelicans, war canoes, medicine men, suns, caribou, sea monsters, and other figures — probably had a religious or magical significance.

"Paddle up closer," urged Belva. "I want to see the paintings better."

On the cliff face, near the arrow rock, were a moose, a crane, a disc shape, horned human figures, a gnome-like figure, and a sturgeon in a net.

After sitting awhile in silence, admiring these creations of the past, we continued on through the lake.

"Look — a mink!" Harvi exclaimed. He pointed to a sleek dark head in front of us, which trailed an ever-widening V in the water. We watched as the mink reached shore and shook himself. The water sparkled like a shattered spectrum as it flew from his coat. He scampered around some boulders and then came back to sit on his haunches and stare at us as we paddled by.

We passed Millstone Rock, a flat table of rock resting on a ledge, long used as a camping spot by early travelers. Here David Thompson "At 6³⁰ PM put up on a smooth Rock — dark cloudy Day — with mizzling Rain — Killed 1 Duck."

As we neared the entrance of Thursday Bay, the sun sank behind a

115

ridge. Trembling skeins of geese, heading south, were silhouetted in the magenta afterglow. We landed on a small island opposite the bay and made camp in the evening coolness.

The voyageurs, after having paddled since dawn, would also stop for the night just at dusk. To make camp they would pile the cargo neatly on shore, covering it with a tarp, and carefully place the upturned canoe nearby. Then they would build a fire and hang a kettle of water over it from a tripod of poles. If a bourgeois were along, they would erect his tent, preferably under a pine on a flat moss-covered ledge.

Garry described his tent: "in the short space of a quarter of an Hour your Inn is prepared. Our tent is about 30 Feet by 15, of Canvas, handsomely striped in Paint on the Top. An oil cloth is placed as a Carpet at the Bottom . . . Our boxes and our Casettes become our Chairs & Tables. After supper all this is cleared and our Beds are spread. First, Canvas which forms the Cover of the Bed and our Seat in the Canoe. Then a Bed of Blankets sewn together which form an Article of Trade in the Interior; on these two fine Blankets as Sheets and above this a coloured Blanket as a Coverlid."

Our camp was much simpler. The lone upturned metal canoe rested on shore. We pitched the small white tent under sheltering Norways on a bed of balsam boughs. Just inside were our few packs and behind them were spread the sleeping bags. A pot of coffee bubbled over a small fire in the crevice of a rock ledge jutting over the lake.

Supper finished and pipes lit, the voyageurs would gather around the fire for jesting and horseplay. After their fun they would roll up in blankets on a bed of rock under the canoes. As they slept, the bourgeois in his tent would scratch impressions of the day's journey in his leatherbound diary. Restive after writing and a day of inactivity in the canoe, he would walk down to the shore to enjoy the sounds of his wilderness encampment. There, under an indigo sky sequined with stars, he would listen to the soft windsongs of the pines, to the washing of water on the rocks, to the *jug-o-rums* of bullfrogs in the swamp across the bay, to the steady hum of the mosquito, to the mournful cry of the loon.

This night as we sat around the fire, I felt like a bourgeois. But instead

116

of writing or listening to the night sounds as they had, I wanted to hear what our diarists had written about today's trip.

"Tonight we start with Delafield," I said, looking for my notes. As I began reading, Harvi moved closer to listen. Why, I didn't know. On other nights he had seemed splendidly preoccupied with other tasks.

"Wednesday, July 23. Clear and pleasant. Breakfast before embarking in order to allow the tents &c. to dry, as well as the portage from Lac Bois Blanc, the baggage always receiving some injury passing a wet portage, from the bushes. This lake discharges itself into the next by two rivers; one about a mile N.E. from the portage, the other at the portage. The fall at the portage is the handsomest I have seen this side of the Height of Land. It is about a hundred yards wide, emptying a great body of water over a fall of about 15 feet, and then a rapid some feet more. This is called the Petit Bois Blanc Portage & Rapid. In a few ensuing miles am obliged to make three more portages, to avoid the rapids of this furious stream, which is increased by the junction of the other river or outlet from Lac Bois Blanc. The first is called the Great Tree Portage, and is a granite rock formation. From this run two rapids of about seven feet descent to the Point of Woods Portage, distant three miles from the last. Descent about 8 feet. This river of communication has divided into three, since I left Bois Blanc Portage. Two of them unite before passing the Point of Woods Portage. The third is called the Rock Portage of Crooked Lake, and is about 200 feet long over a granite ridge. The descent about twenty feet. A stream is tumbling in from the S. just below these falls which I have no doubt is the junction of the third branch before noticed. Thus in the course of 6 or 7 miles I have passed four portages and descended between 60 & 70 feet, loading & reloading the canoe and carrying the luggage as many times on the men's backs. A narrow strait with high granitic ridges on the sides and of deep water leads us to the Crooked Lake. . . . Pass into the Crooked Lake. Observe a smoke on an island as we enter. The crew commence their chant & it draws out a band of Indians, boys and girls, in all 20. In the group we discover a red cap of the voyageur & approach at his hail. He proves to be one of Mr. Thompson's men. He had been taken sick on the Grand Portage & was left behind. I give him a pas-

117

sage &c., buying a paddle for him of the Indians at the expense of a plug of tobacco.

"Crooked Lake is entirely filled with islands. We are once more lost. The afternoon very temperate and calm but my guide not knowing where he is, I make an early encampment. The old water levels are distinctly marked on the rocky islands of this lake. At some time the lake level appears to have been 3½ feet higher than at present. There are several intermediate lines, denoting other levels at other times. Throughout this day's journey the granitic formations have prevailed. At the Bois Blanc Portage the granite and green stone were in junction. Some of the intermediate portages were of granite. The islands in Crooked Lake are principally of granite and slope into the lake. Green stone occurs rather in masses than in veins, in this neighborhood, associating rather than alternating with the granite. The cliff where the arrows are is a fine example of it. . . .

"Thursday, July 24. Embark again on Crooked Lake shortly after sun rise. Conclude to return to the Indians for a guide over this lake, and when on the way meet with a hunting party and take one of them along as guide. He, together with a boy 10 or 11 years old, accompanies us in their little canoe of about 10 feet, and are able to keep ahead of my canoe with its seven paddles. The Indians use very wide blade paddles, and the North canoemen very small ones. The Indian paddles slowly & the Canadian quickly. My old guide is much mortified that another should be employed, but it would have been very strange had he known the track thro' this well-named lake, not having been here for twenty years. The islands of Crooked Lake that I saw were all granite. They were sloping into the lake and none of them high. The diminution of the rock formations seems to be gradual from the Height of Land, Westward. In some of the granite rocks observed masses of green stone imbedded, some round, others angular, forming a sort of breccia; but they were not numerous enough to give this name to the formation. They were, of course, contemporaneous with the granite."

Harvi got up to put another stick of wood on the fire as I began reading Bigsby.

"A series of violent rapids and cascades, from three to five miles long, now follow, with their portages. Of the first, the reader is presented with

118

a view. At the lower end of one of these rapids there is an interesting relic of ancient Indian warfare in a hollow pile of stones, five feet broad by six long. It is now only three feet high, and has an aperture in the side, by which the rapids below may be watched. Each stone of the ground-tier (granite and gneiss) would require the united strength of three to four men to move it. Under this shelter, in days now gone by, the Chippewas, or Wood Indians, used to watch for their invaders, the Sioux of the plains, — a race of horsemen and warriers living principally on buffalo.

"We next came to a narrow of still water, the entrance in fact of Lake Croche (crooked), about twenty miles long. . . .

"Seven miles from the upper end of the lake, the passage is almost closed by large blocks and bowlders; but not far from thence, westerly, the lake widens, and becomes diversified by fine islands, and an occasional high white hummock on the main. Some square masses of bleached rock dotting the shore made me think I beheld a Canadian village.

"In the middle of the lake, where the islands were thickest, we shot past a pretty and unexpected sight.

"We saw, sitting before a conical wigwam, a handsome, comfortably-dressed young Indian and his wife at work, a child playing with pebbles on the shore, and a fox-like dog keeping watch. There they sat, fearless and secure. When they saw us they only nodded and laughed. It occurred to me that many an Englishman might envy them.

"Heathen though they be, the greatest affection often obtains between husband and wife. An Indian and his wife, I was informed, hunting alone on the plains, were met by a war-party of the Sioux. They endeavoured to escape, but the poor woman was overtaken, struck to the ground, and scalped.

"Seeing this, the husband, although at this time beyond either the balls or arrows of the Sioux, turned, and, drawing his knife, rushed furiously upon them, to revenge the death of his wife, even at the inevitable sacrifice of his own life; but he was shot before he reached the foe. This occurred not long ago."

"Now that was a proper bedtime story," Belva said.

Later I lay in my sleeping bag, unready for sleep. Overhead, moonlight filtered down through the trees and fashioned a shadow filigree of pine wisps and cedar fans on the ceiling of our tent. As I looked at the delicate traceries, I thought of La Vérendrye and Peter Pond and Alexander Mackenzie, perhaps camped on this very point, dreaming of the uncharted beyond, of the Western Sea. I thought of how the same restlessness and spirit of adventure which gripped them, today urges other men to new beyonds, to the sea of space.

It was still and cold. I heard a loon call and waited for the answer almost sure to follow. Instead, a wolf howled from a distant ridge, long and mournfully.

October 10. CROOKED LAKE TO LAC LA CROIX

BEHIND the night-black pines on the far shore, the dawn spread out and, caught in the frayed thread ends of the clouds, flushed cerise. So quickly the colors changed to lavender that it was almost imperceptible. After an instant of blushing gray, the sun pushed through into the full glory of a frosty autumn morning.

We left our sleeping bags as life began to stir outside the tent. A squirrel trilled behind us, a pileated woodpecker flew over with a loud, harsh, rattling cry: "Wake up, wake up."

We sat on the granite ledge, bathed in sunlight, drinking coffee and watching Harvi cook breakfast. He would have no assistance — and needed none. The pungent smoke of the pine-knot fire carried to us the tantalizing smell of bacon curling in near doneness. As we ate breakfast a flock of mallards circled the bay, then flew close over in single file, filling the air with a reedy *quack, quack* and a whistle of wings. White mists on the black water of the lake floated, ran, and swirled in funnels. Wet moss on the rocks around us was a rich, verdant green. Leading out from the little beach below us, we could see through the clear water a heron's tracks, made as he coursed his hungry way across the ripple rows in the golden sand.

After breaking camp we set off through the bendings and windings of Crooked Lake. Successive cloud masses, dark and leaden, intermittently covered the sun. The air became chill, and it felt like snow.

Soon large flakes bombarded us. Many times as the clouds raced over, we were snowed on while distant islands and shores were highlighted by the sun. Then came rain squalls and hail, beating a steady staccato on the metal canoe (and on our heads too!) while it churned the water into a froth.

"What a hell of a time to be canoeing," Harvi complained.

"No, Harvi," Belva remonstrated. "It's fun." Then she suddenly cried, "Look, another eagle!"

From the shadows, just before the skies cleared, we saw a bright rainbow arching across the black sky ahead, one end in the water and the other on a rocky pine-covered island. Under the rainbow a bald eagle swooped toward us as though to observe such queer late intruders into his domain. He evidently considered us of no consequence, for he veered upwards and continued his soaring and searching. We had seen many eagles on the trip, but this was the most memorable.

We continued our meandering course through Crooked Lake, between cliffs and islands, through narrow channels, and finally came to Curtain Falls (Le Rideau). There the water from Crooked Lake flows over a hundred-foot-wide ledge in a twenty-foot drop.

Before starting over the portage, we left our packs and scrambled down the outcrop of rock below the falls. We stood in awe on the primitive granite, assailed by the savage roaring and brushed by the spray that, carried in wild eddies of air, formed rainbow fans in the mist above the falls. We watched the water fall in a smooth, black, liquid curtain to break into a tumultuous, foaming mass that pushed frantically in a succession of three rapids between rock walls into Iron Lake. Then we climbed back up the rocks, picked up our packs, and continued over the portage.

122

Following the path along the steep rocky bank, we caught glimpses of the mad green water below, but its roar was deadened by the wet fallen leaves and the dense forest. A red squirrel in the branches overhead warned us with an explosive trill that we were in his territory. Then, in a tail-jerking, foot-stamping fury, he lashed out at us with a hiccup-punctuated chirring. When we paid no attention, his rage subsided to a petulant sputter. He ducked, still sputtering, into a hole for cover when an errant cloud momentarily obscured the sun and spattered a few drops of rain. The drops clung to the tips of multicolored leaves and sparkled like jewels in the rain-washed streams of sunlight. We came to the end of the portage and dropped the canoe into a foam-flecked pool at the bottom of the last rapids.

As we pushed off from shore, I warned Harvi to be careful, for here David Thompson "near upset" on his "Passage out." Then we continued through Iron Lake (3–5 miles) and Bottle Lake (.75 miles) to Bottle portage (Le Flacon), six moderately level muddy rods to Lac la Croix.

Looking out into Lac la Croix from the end of Bottle portage, I wondered how many canoes had loaded here and started out — how much weight in trade goods had been carried over the portages that we had crossed thus far. As I sat on a rock, waiting for Belva and Harvi, I looked among my notes and found a list of the North West Company's posts in the Northwest for 1802.

	Posts	*Partners*	*Clerks*	*Voyageurs*	*Total*
Rainy River (Quetico-Superior posts among these)	6	0	6	28	34
Red & Assiniboine rivers	10	2	16	90	108
Lake Winnipeg	7	2	13	65	80
Fort Dauphin	7	1	14	60	75
Saskatchewan River	9	2	16	80	98
English River	9	2	12	75	89
Athabaska	18	5	16	186	207
Upper Athabaska River	3	2	4	44	50

I took out paper and pencil and began figuring the approximate number of voyageurs and canoes and the weight of the goods. The arithmetic went as follows: total voyageurs listed (628) minus those from Athabaska who came only as far as Rainy Lake (230) gave 398 northmen. Of the

400 pork-eaters at Grand Portage, a third carried goods to the Athabaska House at Rainy Lake. Adding these men to the 398 northmen made a total of *531 voyageurs* on the portages during the season. To find the number of canoes on the lakes, I divided 8, the average number of voyageurs to a north canoe, into 531 and got *66 canoes*. These 66 canoes each carried 35 pieces weighing 90 pounds each, which totaled *104 tons of trade goods!* But wait — I forgot the XY Co., which had a third the number of employees of the North West Company. That must be added too. No wonder the portages were packed hard and the voyageurs frequently had lame backs, hernias, sprained ankles, chafing boils, nausea, and bloody noses.

Lac la Croix, or Lake of the Cross, was known to the Chippewa as Pine Lake or *She-gonne-go-que-ming,* frequently shortened to just *Nequaquon.*

The course through the lake, which is bent back on itself, is twenty-two miles long. The lake has long extensions to the Maligne, the Namakan, and the Loon Rivers. The shores are rugged and deeply forested. It is a lake with abrupt projections of rock: massive cliffs, dangerous reefs, and more than 250 islands. It passes from low country in the east across a big stretch of open water to higher shores in the west.

Winding our way through the southeast arm of Lac la Croix, we passed the island, "just off the main," which held the round tower mentioned by Bigsby, and stopped a few minutes at Warrior Hill on Irving Island. An immense granite hill rising steeply from the shore, it was used by early Chippewa warriors in tests of endurance. From here a short run along the west shore of the island took us to the Painted Rocks.

It was snowing again, softly and quietly. In the snow-blurred distance, the islands floated in a sea of flakes and mist. The hinterlands receded into planes of lighter gray. The pines were growing whiter and whiter.

The sheer cliff of the Painted Rocks, rising a hundred feet from the water's edge and running two hundred and fifty feet at its base, consists of sharp angular masses of granite covered with green, bronze, orange, and black lichens.

Lichens, or *tripe de roche,* were eaten by the voyageurs to fend off starvation during periods of want. First they had to boil them into a glue-like mass. Radisson explained: "upon these rocks we find some shells, blackish w^{th}out and ye inner part whitish by reason of the heat of the sun

124

& of the humidity. They are in a manner glued to the rock; so we must gett another stone to gett them off by scraping hard. The kittle was full wth the scraping of the rocks, wch soone after it boyled became like starch, black and clammie & easily to be swallowed."

On the face of the cliff, a man's height above the water line, were brick-red paintings. The largest collection known to exist in North America, they are not mentioned by any of the early travelers.

As our canoe edged closer, we could see them all — a little smoking man, tracks leading to an hourglass figure, three moose, a warrior group, the symbols L R 1781 scratched white on the granite, and hand prints spread over a large area. The Chippewas say a water manitou drew the pictures many years ago. Harvi splashed water on them with his paddle, making the colors as vivid as if freshly painted. As we rocked in the canoe, submerged in a sea of whiteness, I would not have been surprised if the manitou himself had risen from the depths in anger, commanding us to move on.

We made our way around Coleman Island to the big stretch, where we camped on a small island.

Just as Belva and I finished erecting the tent, Harvi shouted, "They're Minnesota brown." This was his way of saying the fish were done. In a special fishing hole nearby, he had caught three walleyes, steaked them, and fried them to a golden brown. Beside the pan of sizzling fish, a large pot of coffee bubbled and steamed.

"Nothing can beat this, not steak or duck, not even the voyageur's favorite dish," I muttered between mouthfuls.

"What did they like?" asked Harvi, as he bent to make *his* favorite dish — two slices of buttered bread with a fried walleye steak between.

"Rubbaboo," I answered. "Peter Jacobs gave the recipe." After explaining that Peter Jacobs was a young Indian convert brought to Rainy Lake in 1839 by the Reverend James Evans, "the Apostle of the North," to carry on missionary work, I read his recipe. "After I had got the wood in order, and made a good blazing fire, I took my kettle, went to the lake, and put in it about two quarts of water. While this was getting to boil over the fire I took a two-quart hand dish half full of water, and put into it some flour, and stirred it till it looked like *mush*. The pan was now full.

125

As the water in the kettle was now boiling, I took my pandish, and put all that was in it in the kettle, where it became thinner. I then took a stick and stirred. This, of course, took some time to boil. When it boiled I kept stirring it in order to prevent the dregs of the flour soup (if I may so call it) from sinking and sticking at the bottom of the kettle and burning. If it burned the dinner would be spoiled. This frequently happens with bad and indolent cooks. I myself succeeded very well, as I was determined to be a good cook on this occasion. All depends upon the faithful continuance of stirring the flour-soup with a stick, until such time as it is cooked. I carefully attended to this. When the flour soup was quite cooked, I removed the kettle from the fire, and while my soup was boiling hot I jumped at my hatchet or tomahawk, and cut to pieces about a pound weight of *pemmican*, after which I threw this into the kettle. I stirred this quickly, so that the grease of the *pemmican* might be dissolved in the hot flour-soup. Thus ends the cooking. The time it takes to cook this is less than half an hour."

"Thus ends rubbaboo for me." Belva wrinkled her nose. "That recipe sounds as horrible as the name."

"I'd rather have walleye," Harvi added, finishing his sandwich and moving closer. "Aren't you going to read the diaries tonight?"

This came as a pleasant surprise to me — Harvi's asking me to read the diaries. But, as I thought about it, I really shouldn't have been surprised at all. Lac la Croix has been his stamping ground for nearly thirty years. During those years he has come to know every pine tree and rock shoal on the lake.

"Here, take the notes, Harvi," I said proudly — proudly, because now, in his favorite haunt, some of my enthusiasm for the past had rubbed off on him. "You can do the honors tonight."

The ground was wet from the snow. Our pine-knot fire burned furiously and the snow hissed as it hit the flames. Harvi began reading Bigsby.

"After some sharp currents along narrows, and the picturesque Iron Lake (three miles and two-thirds across), we arrive at the Pewarbic, or Bottle Portage, and Lake Lacroix.

"The Lake of the Cross is thirty-four miles long by eighteen wide, ac-

126

cording to Mackenzie. According to our survey, it contains 260 islands, often pine-tufted with rushy sides, besides rocks innumerable.

"Its shores are extremely capricious in their outlines, and often bare and high. The Indians have names for most of the localities, but we could seldom procure them.

"Wild rice grows so abundantly and fine on the south shore of Lake Lacroix that we sometimes could hardly push our canoes through it. Its water-lilies are superb, much the finest I have seen. They are about the size of a dahlia, for which they might be taken. They are double throughout, every row of petals diminishing by degrees, and passing gradually from the purest white to the highest lemon-colour. There is in the neighboring lakes a variety, wholly bright yellow.

"A few miles from the Pewarbic Portage, on an island near the south main, there are the remains of a round tower, or defensive building of some sort, twenty-seven feet in diameter. It was erected by the Indians, and commands a wide view of expanses and woody isles.

"The new or Dog-River route, from Lake Superior to the Lake of the Woods, enters Lake Lacroix on its north-east side by the River Maligne, and thenceforwards is the same as the old route."

"Harvi, the rice still isn't that thick, is it?" Belva asked.

"No," he answered. "But there is still some." Then he went on to read Delafield. "The portage from Crooked Lake is one post over a granite ridge. The fall is called by the Frenchmen the Window Curtain Fall. It is a handsome shoot, 35 feet descent. Immediately after making this portage, run three rapids, descent about 5 feet. The course thro' the strait connecting Crooked Lake with Lac l'Croix is very circuitous, and after following it 7 or 8 miles come to the Bottle Portage. It is of one full post and leads to Lac l'Croix. Keep the Indian guide 'til we arrive at that part of Lac l'Croix where the New Road joins the Old, when my guide discharges his debt by giving the Indian a blanket in addition to the pay in provisions which I had given him, to his great satisfaction, for the job. My crew were all rejoiced to be upon the New Road & from the complaints I had heard of the old, and pains and labors witnessed, I confess I felt the elation also, as if some change for the better was at hand; but it all proved the character of the Canadian. The change was no other ways

127

in our favor than that we were advanced upon the journey and near to larger lakes. To complain of the present and sigh for the past and the future, is the common custom of this weather beaten clan. Encamp at sun set on the beach of an island affording a sufficient level for my tent, a luxury that I had not enjoyed for three nights, my encampment having been on sloping or curved rocks that did not allow a bed at full length. The comfort of a good night's rest, with limbs at full length without molestation, I can ascribe to the benefits of the New Road. Feeling the want of a change of diet I have some rice boiled, which with a pair of ducks that my Indian guide shot, makes an excellent supper. The ducks are roasted voyageur fashion by splitting them, and extending the parts on a forked stick which is stuck in the dirt by the fire! They roast quickly and well in this way. Fresh fish cooked in the same way is very good. The Frenchmen roast and eat the entrails &c. of the ducks as a great relish.

"In the evening, showers. . . .

"The granite of this neighborhood is without mica as usual, altho it occurs as if accidentally in a few instances. A rock approaching coarse mica slate or a micaceous schist begins to appear here associated with granite.

"The junction of the New and the Old Road in this lake is also of interest because we again strike the Boundary Line, or direct communication, as supposed. Leaving the Old Road in Lake Saganaga by the River Saganaga the Line joins the New Road in Sturgeon Lake, and thence by the River Malin to Lac l'Croix where the two routes meet. Knife Lake, Bois Blanc Lake and Crooked Lake are therefore within the jurisdiction of the U.S.

"Friday, July 25. The apparent approach of a storm delays embarkation til 7 a.m. when I start in hope of arriving at the portage from Lac l'Croix before the rain commences. Four Indian canoes pass me whilst embarking, the two hinder ones only discover me. They approach, but I leave them without much parley. This is the third band of Indians that I have met since I left Lake Superior. Another Indian & his squaw soon after overtake me to trade & are disappointed. They were civil & well disposed. Had a pack in their canoe. A canoe from the North soon after passes, on its way to Fort William. Mr. Nelson, an Hudson's Bay Compy clerk from his post near the Winnepec (I think), was the Bourgeois. . . .

"Mr. Nelson told me that he had met Mr. Ferguson on the River l'Pluie, going to the Lake of the Woods. He kindly waits whilst I write a letter in my canoe for home.

"The rock formations undergo a change in Lac l'Croix. The granite alternates with a micaceous slaty rock that is the mica schist of some. It is stratified and lies with a dip to the N. of various degrees & sometimes as much as 45°. It is in ranges that run near E & W."

"Harvi, you've been hiding a talent from us," Belva said. "You read that beautifully."

I applauded and said, "Why don't you read tomorrow night too?"

Harvi dismissed the compliment with a characteristic shrug, and went to secure the canoe for the night.

I sat idly watching the snow disappear into the spluttering fire. I was faced with a big decision: whether to go to bed or to get some wood. Belva showed no such hesitancy. "I'm going to bed," she said with conviction. "I'm tired. 'Nor Ghosts, nor Rattlesnakes, nor Spiders,' as Garry said, 'nothing can prevent the fatigued Voyageur from sleeping.'" I decided I'd go to bed too. So did Harvi.

October 11. LAC LA CROIX TO
BARE PORTAGE ON NAMAKAN LAKE

Our day began cold and gray. The pines and cedars drooped under a burden of heavy wet snow, and a sullen sky threatened even worse. Over the dull black water a flotilla of stranded clouds maneuvered in foggy formations that obscured the near shore.

The only cheerful note in the dismal day was the orange flame of our fire. We huddled around it — three weatherbound voyageurs in waterproof parkas — absorbing its toasty warmth and toasting each other, in true voyageur fashion, with the equal warmth of our toddies. We were in no hurry to leave the comparative comfort of our camp for the shivering discomfort of an aluminum canoe on a cold, murky lake.

"The wood's gone," Harvi commented, as he stirred the fire and added the last piece of driftwood to the glowing coals.

"I'll get some more," I volunteered heroically.

I regretted my rash act when I found myself walking through the sodden forest to find a place where dry wood might lie in some protected corner. Distracted by the swirling movements of the fog on the lake, I sat for a while beneath a great pine and studied them. Then I gazed northeast where the turbulent waters of the Maligne enter Lac la Croix. Remembering the heat of the summer sun on our trips up the Maligne to Sturgeon Lake, I soon forgot the cold.

130

As I gazed, the vaporous outlines of bark canoes took shape in the swirling fog. They appeared out of the past carrying the dim figures of early adventurers, silent and shrouded in mist — dim figures of the succession of adventurers who had also journeyed over these waters; for this was the last section of the Kaministikwia waterway from Fort William before it joined the Grand Portage route here in Lac la Croix. My memory filled in the details of when, why, and who they were.

Jacques de Noyon led the way in 1688. Starting up the Kaministikwia River from Lake Superior, he went on to Dog Lake, Lac des Mille Lacs, Pickerel Lake, Sturgeon Lake, and the Maligne, in search of new fur-trade areas. This voyageur was the first recorded white man to penetrate the Northwest through the Quetico-Superior to Rainy Lake.

After de Noyon, other French traders and would-be explorers followed over the waterway until 1732, when La Vérendrye began using the Grand Portage route. During the succeeding seventy-two years nobody used the road until 1804. In that year the Nor'Westers began pouring over it to continue their activities in the Northwest until their company was absorbed into the Hudson's Bay Company in 1821.

Then Hudson's Bay Company officials from Montreal used the route. One of the first of these was Nicholas Garry, as mentioned earlier, on his assignment to bring the Nor'Westers into the Hudson's Bay Company. The most prominent of these officials was George Simpson. As governor of the Northern Department from 1821, and governor-in-chief from 1826, he made many long, hazardous, speedy trips throughout the Northwest. During these numerous tours of inspection, he fashioned and welded the new monopoly of the Hudson's Bay Company into a great fur empire. Until his death in 1860, the "little emperor," with unbounded energy and pomp, made almost yearly trips over the Kaministikwia to the Red River and beyond.

In 1816 the advance guard of civilization began appearing over the Kaministikwia, frequently in the company of fur trade officials. On their way to settle the Canadian West, they relied on voyageur-manned canoes for transportation. As their numbers increased, small steam tugs towed the canoes in fleets across larger bodies of water.

Heading the procession were the Red River pastors — Reverend Pierre

131

Antoine Tabeau in 1816, and two years later, the Reverends Joseph Norbert Provencher, Sévère Dumoulin, and William Edge. At the Red River settlements these Roman Catholic priests resumed and enlarged upon the missionary work begun earlier by the Jesuits in the Lake Superior region. They aided Lord Selkirk's colony by discouraging the aggressions of the Roman Catholic French-Canadian voyageurs, who were the employees of the colony's great rival, the North West Company. They also aided the establishment of a Roman Catholic hierarchy, so important to the French-Canadians in British-held Protestant Canada.

The first mass migration of French-Canadians followed the Red River pastors in 1819–1820, once they were sure that they could receive spiritual succor in established Roman Catholic churches.

In 1823 boundary commissioners from Canada and the United States canoed up and down sections of the route.

Also in 1823, Major Stephen H. Long, under order of the United States Department of War, led an expedition to determine where the 49th parallel lay. This line had been designated by the Convention of 1818 as the boundary west of Lake of the Woods. Long's party, which included soldiers, a geologist, a zoologist, an artist, and an astronomer, was also instructed to gather as much information as possible about the region drained by the Minnesota and Red Rivers. Starting up the Minnesota River and crossing the Height of Land, the party proceeded down the Red River. After the 49th parallel had been located and a solid oak post had been driven into the ground to mark the point where the boundary crossed the Red River, the expedition started home, returning by way of the Kaministikwia route.

Seven years later a bit of impressionable femininity sped over the Kaministikwia on a honeymoon trip. Frances Simpson had just married her famous cousin, George Simpson, in London. On this trip, Fort Frances, the Hudson's Bay fort on Rainy River, was named in her honor.

In the decade after 1830 both Roman Catholic and Protestant missionaries traveled through on their way west to convert the Indians to Christianity and to minister to the spiritual needs of new settlers. Georges Antoine Belcourt came in 1831 to fill the vacancy left by Dumoulin. In 1839 the Reverend Francis Norbert Blanchet and the Reverend Modest Demers were headed for Oregon territory, where they would become prominent Roman Catholic bishops. The same year Wesleyan missionaries, the Reverends James Evans, Peter Jacobs, Thomas Hurlburt, Henry Steinham, and William Masson were on their way to Rainy Lake and Norway House, their mission headquarters. Evans, the "Apostle of the North," made many native converts, even in far-off Athabaska.

The famous Canadian artist, Paul Kane, accompanied Sir George Simpson to Fort Edmonton in 1846, sketching Indians and scenery along the way.

The following year two big-game hunters, Frederick Ulric Graham and Vincent Corbet, went with Sir George to Edmonton. A year after that, surgeon and naturalist Sir John Richardson used this route on his third trip to the Arctic. He had previously accompanied Sir John Franklin's polar expeditions. In 1857 Hind, Dawson, and Palliser began their explorations of the country between Lake Superior and the Red River settlements. Two years later Robert Kennicott came through in a brigade of three Hudson's Bay Company canoes on his way to undertake the first American scientific exploration of the Yukon. After spending three years on his expedition, the brilliant young naturalist returned with many specimens of birds and animals to be added to the collection in the Smithsonian Institution. The detailed observations in his journal of the physical aspects of Alaska aided the United States in deciding to acquire the territory in 1867.

In 1869 the Riel rebellion at the Red River settlements brought fourteen hundred soldiers under the command of Colonel Garnet Wolseley. As they traveled over the Kaministikwia, they actually built the Dawson Road, and Captain Guy L. Huysche, a member of Wolseley's staff, wrote a fascinating account of the expedition.

Finally, during the decade 1870–1880, immigrants of all ages, seeking new lives in the Canadian West, used the Dawson Road in ever-increasing numbers. One distinguished traveler was George M. Grant. He went through in 1876 as secretary to the expedition led by Sandford Fleming, engineer-in-chief to the Dominion government. They were making a tour of inspection in the West preliminary to construction of the transcontinental railroad promised British Columbia when it joined the Dominion.

October 11

N.W. CO. FORT
Fort Frances
H.B. CO. FORT
FORT ST. PIERRE

A.F. CO. FORT
International Falls

Rainy Lake

Bare P.

Tar Point

Namakan R.

Namakan L.

PAINTED High
ROCK Falls

Sand
Point L.

Dawson P.

Lac La Croix

Beatty P.

BOURASSA POST
N.W. CO. POST
H.B. CO.

Loon R.

Loon L.

Vermilion R.

France R.

Loon Falls P.

Vermilion L.

↓ To St. Louis R.
and Fond du lac

Another was Peter O'Leary who visited the New World in 1874 to give "an honest opinion from

A WORKINGMAN'S STANDPOINT

on these countries as fields of emigration for those of the toiling masses" desiring to leave the United Kingdom.

As these figures receded into the mists again, my mind returned to our trips, in other years, up the Maligne. Carrying our packs across Isle portage at Twin Falls, we had pointed the prow of our canoe upstream through the swirls and smooth black slicks of the Maligne.

All along the river, we found evidence left by those who had built and used the Dawson Road. We inspected the dams, especially those at Twin Falls. Now all that remains of these dams is rotting squared timbers and rusty iron spikes. The dams, by raising the water level, made much of the river navigable for steam tugs. We kicked away the duff on some of the portage trails, exposing stretches of corduroy road used to cover swampy or muddy places. We saw pieces of anchor chain rusting on the river's edge and, at the fourth and fifth portages, lying on the river's bottom a few feet from shore, a rusty, broken propeller, a boiler head, and an old steam tug boiler.

These tell of a decade of hard travel and bring the past very near. Less tangible, but equally important in bringing the past closer, are the descriptions and incidents recorded in the diaries of some of the travelers over the route.

Now our *compagnons du voyage* over the Grand Portage route will be joined by others of more recent date — those traveling the Kaministikwia route west of Lake Superior.

"Arnold!" I heard Belva calling. "Where's our wood? The fire's almost out."

Picking up an armful of sticks, I hastened back to hear her asking Harvi, "Where do you suppose he is *this* time?"

"Probably dreaming up a side trip to the Maligne," he answered.

"When it's so cold?" Belva objected. "I'd rather just sit here by the fire and read about it."

Harvi agreed with her.

I put some wood on the fire and sat down. "It *is* pretty nice by the fire. A proxy trip will have to do, I guess. It's two against one, anyway."

"Eavesdropper," Belva chided.

Harvi started to the lake for water. "Good. I'll brew up another pot of coffee; then you start reading."

"You two sure made up my mind in a hurry," I acquiesced. "Let's start at Sturgeon and go down river to Isle portage."

"Read Hind's description of Sturgeon first," Belva said.

"No lake yet seen on the route can bear comparison for picturesque scenery with Sturgeon Lake. The numerous deep bays, backed by high-wooded hills or rocks, rugged or smooth, according to their aspects, its sudden contraction into a river breadth for a few yards between large islands and the equally abrupt breaking out into open stretches of water, offered a constant and most pleasing variety of scene. The high jutting points of granite rock, which here and there confine the channel, offer rare opportunities for beholding on one side an intricate maze of island scenery, and on the other an open expanse of lake, with deep and gloomy bays, stretching seemingly into the dark forest as far as the eye can reach.

"Here we met several Ojibways in their elegant birch bark canoes. They were very friendly, and apparently delighted with a small present of tobacco and tea. One young hunter with his squaw hurried to the shore as we approached, but soon returned gaudily painted with patches of vermilion on his cheeks and in bars across his forehead."

"I think Sturgeon is a beautiful lake. Hind apparently did too," Belva commented, as she changed her position by the fire. "What's next?"

"O'Leary not only liked the lake, but he described its inhabitants at the outlet into the Maligne," I continued.

"We crossed Sturgeon Lake . . . The passage was a beautiful one to

MALINE PORTAGE,

where there were several more wigwams. The scenery here was very grand: the rocks thrown about in the greatest confusion; the magnificent sheet of water stretching out before us as far as the eye could reach, with the Indians in their bark canoes engaged in fishing; the wigwams here and there among the trees with their wild and savage-looking inmates

136

standing round; the dense woods in every direction, with the various tints and colours of the foliage; and above all the rich glowing sunset made up a scene that would gladden the heart of a Royal Academician."

"Royal Academician or not, it would mine," asserted Belva.

"Were there any early trading posts on Sturgeon?" Harvi asked.

"The only reference I could ever find was to a Germain Maugenest. John Kipling of the Hudson's Bay Company wrote of him in the Gloucester House Journal on July 10, 1779."

". . . At 10 A.M. came here a French Trader with One Englishman (a John Coates) with 7 Canadians two Indian Chiefs and one Women for their Guides in two large Canoes with nigh 2000 Beaver on their way for Albany [on Hudson's Bay] and it is not in my power to disswade them from it, they acquainted me that they have been 15 days coming down to this place from the place they Wintered at. The Name of the Lake that the House is on is Sturgeon Lake which is nigh to the Rainy Lake."

"Here's an interesting note I found about this Frenchman and Hudson Bay blankets in the Moose Fort Journals of the Hudson's Bay Company Record Society," I said.

"Germain Maugenest came to London in the autumn of 1779 and discussed terms for entering the Company's service. On his advice several kinds of goods new to the Company were ordered for the trade above Gloucester House, where there was keen competition with the French. Amongst the innovations were Point Blankets which were made for the first time for the Hudson's Bay Company in 1780 by Thomas Empson of Witney, Oxfordshire. The first order consisted of 100 each of 1, 1½, 2, 2½, and 3 points, making a total of 500 Point Blankets. The 'points' were known to every Indian familiar with the Company's competitors as representing the price, e.g., a 2½ point blanket was exchanged for 2½ beavers."

"I almost forgot something," I said, as I turned the page. "Harvi, did you ever make galette on a camping trip?"

"What's that?" he asked dubiously.

"Kennicott felt the same way the first time he was exposed to it," I assured him.

". . . Mr. Hubbard found the nest of a ruffed grouse, containing five eggs. These our cooks used in making our galette, thereby giving us quite a treat. This galette is the only form of bread used on a voyage, that is when voyageurs are so fortunate as to have any flour at all. It is made in a very simple style — the flour bag is opened, and a small hollow made in the flour, into which a little water is poured, and the dough is thus mixed in the bag; nothing is added, except perhaps some dirt from the cook's *unwashed* hands with which he kneads it into flat cakes, which are baked before the fire in a frying pan, or cooked in grease. To pampered dyspeptics a breakfast of galette and salt pork might not seem very inviting; but let them try it on a northern voyage, after traveling five hours in the morning without eating, and they will find it otherwise. There is no denying that voyageurs are not apt to be very cleanly, either in their persons or in their cooking; but it is wonderful how any fastidiousness on the subject wears off when a traveler is voyaging in the wilderness."

"Pancake mix is easier," Harvi said with a twinkle in his eye. Then he changed the subject. "Did any of the voyageurs ever shoot the rapids?"

"They sure did," I answered. "Grant told of his ride with them down the first rapid on the river."

"To shoot the rapids in a canoe is a pleasure that comparatively few Englishmen have ever enjoyed, and no picture can give an idea of what it is. There is a fascination in the motion, as of poetry or music, which must be experienced to be understood. The excitement is greater than when on board a steamer, because you are so much nearer the seething water, and the canoe seems such a fragile thing to contend with the mad forces, into the very thick of which it has to be steered. Where the stream begins to descend, the water is an inclined plane, smooth and shining as glare ice. Beyond that it breaks into curling, gleaming rolls which end off in white, boiling caldrons, where the water has broken on the rocks beneath. On the brink of the inclined plane, the motion is so quiet that you think the canoe pauses for an instant. The captain is at the bow, — a broader, stronger paddle than usual in his hand — his eye kindling with enthusiasm, and every nerve and fibre in his body at its utmost tension. The steersman is at his post, and every man is ready. They know that a false stroke, or too weak a turn of the captain's wrist, at the critical moment, means death. A push with the paddles, and, straight and swift as an

138

arrow, the canoe shoots right down into the mad vortex; now into a cross current that would twist her broadside round, but that every man fights against it; then she steers right for a rock, to which she is being resistlessly sucked, and on which it seems as if she would be dashed to pieces; but a rapid turn of the captain's paddle at the right moment, and she rushes past the black mass, riding gallantly as a race horse. The waves boil up at the side threatening to engulf her, but except a dash of spray or the cap of a wave, nothing gets in, and as she speeds into the calm reach beyond, all draw long breaths and hope that another rapid is near."

"I don't understand how they could shoot those rapids." Harvi shook his head. "I'd sure never want to try it."

"But that's not all," I added. "The soldiers of Wolseley's expedition took their big boats down too. Listen to this anonymous report."

"Everyone worked as if for his life; and the wild cries of the Indians, as they shouted directions to each other in their strange language, made those looking on from the shore feel certain that some accident was going to happen; but the cheers and laughter of the crews, as the boats were pulled into smooth water at the foot of the rapids soon dispelled the illusion."

Harvi shook his head again.

"The Indians erected spearing platforms along the river, as well as on the Namakan River," I continued. "George Simpson wrote about them in 1841, as he traveled through on his way around the world, from London to Montreal, Fort Garry, Alaska, California, Siberia, Moscow, and back to London."

"At nearly all the rapids and falls . . . the Indians have erected platforms, which stretch about twenty feet from the shore; and on these they fix themselves, spear in hand, for hours, as silent and motionless as possible, till some doomed fish comes within range of their unerring weapon."

"Those are good spots to fish," Harvi said. "I've caught plenty there myself, but not with a spear."

"Read some more of Tanner's story for Harvi," Belva urged, as she unwound her legs and settled herself again. "It's really weird. It would be unbelievable, if all the other diarists of the period didn't verify it."

"Is he the one Tanner's Lake is named after?" Harvi asked. "The one who was stolen by the Indians?"

I nodded. While looking for the right notes, I explained to Harvi that John Tanner received a near-fatal wound on the river in 1823, while attempting to return to civilization with his two half-breed daughters. After much difficulty in securing the children from the band of Indians with whom they had been living, he started up the river with them and their mother. Preceding him up the river was his assailant-to-be, Ome-zhuh-gwut-oons, who had pretended friendliness. The mishap occurred in a small rapid just below an expansion of the river, later called Tanner's Lake.

". . . At this place the river is about eighty yards wide, and there is, about ten yards from the point before mentioned, a small island of naked rock. I had taken off my coat, and I was, with great effort, pushing up my canoe against the powerful current, which compelled me to keep very near the shore, when the discharge of a gun at my side arrested my progress. I heard a bullet whistle past my head, and felt my side touched, at the same instant that the paddle fell from my right hand, and the hand itself dropped powerless to my side. The bushes were obscured by the smoke of the gun, but at a second look I saw Ome-zhuh-gwut-oons escaping. At that time the screams of my children drew my attention to the canoe, and I found every part of it was becoming covered with blood. I endeavoured, with my left hand, to push the canoe in shore, that I might pursue after him; but the current being too powerful for me, took my canoe on the other side, and threw it against the small rocky island before mentioned. I now got out, pulled the canoe a little on to the rock, with my left hand, and then made an attempt to load my gun. Before I could finish loading, I fainted, and fell on the rock. When I came to myself again, I was alone on the island, and the canoe, with my daughters, was just going out of sight in the river below. Soon after it disappeared, I fainted a second time; but consciousness at length returned.

"As I believed that the man who had shot me was still watching from his concealment, I examined my wounds, and finding my situation desperate, my right arm being much shattered, and the ball having entered my body, in the direction to reach my lungs, and not having passed out, I called to him, requesting him to come, and by putting an immediate end to my life, to release me from the protracted suffering I had in prospect.

140

'You have killed me,' said I; 'but though the hurt you have given me must be mortal, I fear it may be some time before I shall die. Come, therefore, if you are a man, and shoot me again.' Many times I called to him, but he returned me no answer. My body was now almost naked, as I had on, when shot, besides my pantaloons, only a very old and ragged shirt, and much of this had been torn off in the course of the morning. I lay exposed to the sun, and the black and green headed flies, on a naked rock, the greater part of a day in July or August, and saw no prospect before me, but that of a lingering death; but as the sun went down, my hope and strength began to revive, and plunging into the river, I swam across to the other side. When I reached the shore, I could stand on my feet, and I raised the sas-sah-kwi, or war whoop, as a cry of exultation and defiance to my enemy. But the additional loss of blood, occasioned by the exertion in swimming the river, caused me another fainting fit, from which, when I recovered, I concealed myself near the bank, to watch for him. Presently I saw Ome-zhuh-gwut-oons come from his hiding place, put his canoe into the water, embark, and begin to descend the river. He came very near my hiding place, and I felt tempted to make a spring, and endeavour to seize and strangle him in the water; but fearing that my strength might not be sufficient, I let him pass without discovering myself.

"I was now tormented with the most excessive thirst, and as the bank was steep and rocky, I could not, with my wounded arm, lie down to drink. I was therefore compelled to go into the water, and let my body down into it, until I brought my mouth to a level with the surface, and thus I was able to drink. By this time, the evening growing somewhat cooler, my strength was, in part, restored; but the blood seemed to flow more freely. I now applied myself to dressing the wound in my arms. I endeavoured, though the flesh was already much swollen, to replace the fragments of the bone; to accomplish which, I tore in strips the remainder of my shirt, and with my teeth and my left hand I contrived to tie these around my arm, at first loosely, but by degrees tighter and tighter, until I thought it had assumed, as nearly as I could give it, the proper form. I then tied on small sticks, which I broke from the branches of trees, to serve as splints, and then suspended my hand in a string, which passed around my neck. After this was completed, I took some of the bark of a choke

141

cherry bush, which I observed there, and chewing it fine applied it to the wounds, hoping thus to check the flowing of the blood. The bushes about me, and for all the distance between me and the river, were covered with blood. As night came on, I chose a place where was plenty of moss, to lie down on, with the trunk of a fallen tree for my pillow. I was careful to select a place near the river, that I might have a chance of seeing any thing that might pass; also, to be near the water in case my thirst should again become urgent. I knew that one trader's canoe was expected, about this time, to pass this place, on the way towards Red River, and it was this canoe from which I expected relief and assistance. There were no Indians nearer than the village from which Ome-zhuh-gwut-oons had followed me, and he, with my wife and daughters, were the only persons that I had any reason to suppose were within many miles of me.

"I laid myself down, and prayed to the Great Spirit, that he would see and pity my condition, and send help to me, now in time of my distress. As I continued praying, the musquitoes, which had settled on my naked body in vast numbers, and were, by their stings, adding greatly to the torment I suffered, began to rise, and after hovering at a little distance above and around me, disappeared entirely. I did not attribute this, which was so great a relief, to the immediate interposition of a Superior Power, in answer to my prayer, as the evening was, at that time, becoming something cool, and I knew it was entirely the effect of change of temperature. Nevertheless, I was conscious, as I have ever been in times of distress and of danger, that the Master of my life, though invisible, was yet near, and was looking upon me. I slept easily and quietly, but not without interruption. Every time I awoke, I remembered to have seen, in my dream, a canoe with white men, in the river before me.

"It was late in the night, probably after midnight, when I heard female voices, which I supposed to be those of my daughters, not more than two hundred yards from me, but partly across the river. I believed that Ome-zhuh-gwut-oons had discovered their hiding place, and was, perhaps, offering them some violence, as the cry was that of distress; but so great was my weakness, that the attempt to afford them any relief seemed wholly beyond my power. I learned afterwards, that my children, as soon as I fainted and fell on the rock, supposing me dead, had been influenced by their mother to turn the canoe down the river, and exert themselves to make their escape. They had not proceeded far, when the woman steered the canoe into a low point of bushes, and threw out my coat, and some other articles. They then ran on a considerable distance, and concealed themselves; but here it occurred to the woman, that she might have done better to have kept the property belonging to me, and accordingly returned to get it. It was when they came to see these things lying on the shore, that the children burst out crying, and it was at this time that I heard them.

"Before ten o'clock next morning, I heard human voices on the river above me, and from the situation I had chosen, I could see a canoe coming, like that I had seen in my dream, loaded with white men. They landed at a little distance above me, and began to make preparations for breakfast. I knew that this was the canoe belonging to Mr. Stewart, of the Hudson's Bay Company, who, together with Mr. Grant, was expected about this time; and being conscious that my appearance would make a painful impression upon them, I determined to wait until they had breakfasted, before I showed myself to them. After they had eaten, and put their canoe again in the water, I waded out a little distance into the river, to attract their attention. As soon as they saw me, the Frenchmen ceased paddling, and they all gazed at me, as if in doubt and amazement. As the current of the river was carrying them rapidly past me, and my repeated calls, in the Indian language, seemed to produce no effect, I called Mr. Stewart by name, and spoke a few words of English, which I could command, requesting them to come and take me. In a moment their paddles were in the water, and they brought the canoe so near where I stood, that I was able to get into it."

When I had finished, I told Harvi that Mr. Stewart and Mr. Grant took Tanner to one of the fur posts on Rainy River, searching along the way for his enemy, Ome-zhuh-gwut-oons, and his wife, who had been guilty of aiding in his attempted murder. Tanner made no further mention of his enemy in the narrative, but he did find his wife detained at the fort with his two daughters. He asked only that she be sent from the post without provisions, and never allowed to return. During the winter he received medical attention from Dr. McLoughlin, and left in the spring for Mackinac to join three of his children who had previously been taken out. His son and two daughters remained with the Indians in the woods.

"I'll sure remember that story every time I make the portage!" Harvi said emphatically.

"Here's the last note. It's Grant again, describing lunch at Isle portage before crossing Lac la Croix."

"Here a steam launch is stationed; and though the engineer thought it a frightful day to travel in, he got ready at our request, but said he could not go four miles an hour as the rain would keep the boiler wet the whole time. We dined with M—'s party, under the shelter of their upturned canoe, on tea and the fattest of fat pork, which all ate with delight unspeakable, for everyone had in himself the right kind of sauce. The day, and our soaked condition, suggested a little brandy as a specific; but their bottle was exhausted, and, an hour before, they had passed round the cork for each to have a smell at. Such a case of 'potatoes and point' moved our pity, and the chief did what he could for them. The Indians excited our admiration; — soaked through, and overworked as they had been, the only word that we heard, indicating that they were conscious of anything unusual, was an exclamation from Baptiste, as he gave himself a shake, — 'Boys, wish I was in a tavern now, I'd get drunk in less than tree hours, I guess.'

"At two o'clock, the steam launch was ready, and, about the same time, the sky cleared a little; a favourable wind, too, sprang up, and though there were showers or heavy mists all the time, the launch towed us the twenty-four miles of Lake Nequaquon [Lac la Croix] in three and a quarter hours."

"We're back in la Croix now," Harvi said, getting up to loosen the tent ropes, "and it looks like we can get going."

The sky had become less ominous. Veiled sunlight poured through the thinning overcast, warming the air and driving the fog from the lake. It lifted our spirits too.

The canoe loaded, we started west across the big stretch of Lac la Croix, now following both the Kaministikwia and the Grand Portage routes, for from Lac la Croix west, they are the same.

The junction of the two routes was marked by Pointe du Mai, long a famous land mark at the east end of Lac la Croix. Our camp of last night

144

was close to this point, perhaps the same one where Macdonell "Killed a cub Bear . . . and slept in sight of the *Mai*."

Here the flow of traffic eastward changed when the Nor'Westers began using the Kaministikwia to Lake Superior. On his return trip in 1803, Henry the younger marked the change: "In Lac la Croix, at Pointe du Mai we struck away from the Grand Portage route, steering on E. course to the left just when we had overtaken an X.Y. brigade steering on the old track to Grand Portage, where they continue to hold their general rendezvous."

The *Mai* was a maypole, or lobstick, used as a landmark on a headland or promontory, or, more frequently, to honor a passenger of importance. The voyageurs made them by cutting away all but a few branches of a pine, leaving only a tuft at the top. In former times such poles dotted the water trails of the north.

Robert Kennicott wrote of his lob on Lac la Croix: "A tall pine, standing out on a point in the lake was climbed by one of the voyageurs, who, with an ax, cut off all the branches, excepting a tuft at the top, thus rendering it very conspicuous. As we paddled off it was saluted with three cheers and the discharge of guns, we, of course, being expected to acknowledge the compliment by a treat (of high wines) at the first opportunity [the real reason for the ceremony]."

Frances Simpson's *Mai* was a fancy one. A lady passenger's visit always made the voyageurs outdo themselves (especially when she was the governor's wife!). She wrote: "mine (being a memorable one) was honored with a red feather, and streamers of purple riband tied to a poll, and fastened to the top of the Tree . . . the surrounding trees were then cut down, in order to leave it open to the Lake. Bernard (the Guide) then presented me with a Gun, the contents of which I discharged against the Tree, and Mr. Miles engraved my name, and the date, on the trunk, so that my 'Lopped Stick' will be conspicuous as long as it stands, among the number of those to be seen along the banks of different Lakes and Rivers."

Halfway across the traverse we stopped for a *pipe*. This was, like the *posé* on a portage, a rough measurement of distance used by the voyageurs. They estimated the length of a lake or stream by the number of times they stopped to rest and smoke. After paddling an hour or more, the guide would shout "Allumez." Then paddles were rested on knees, pipes were filled and lit with flint and steel. After the last puff the order was given to start. Again paddles flashed and a song was started as the canoe moved on.

While I sat enjoying my "pipe," I pictured Sir George Simpson who had crossed the lake so many times. In high beaver hat he sped across this same traverse of Lac la Croix in an express canoe manned by a corps of twelve hand-picked voyageurs — "des hommes choisis! les plus beaux chanteurs du monde!" — the chosen men! the most beautiful singers in the world! The shrill notes of a Highland tune played by his bagpiper, a Scottish import, echoed and re-echoed from the rocky shores of the lake. When the skirling of the pipes droned to a halt, the voices of his crew swelled in song and gradually grew fainter in the distance.

As we wound our way among the islands west of the big stretch, I asked Harvi, "Have you ever heard how the lake got its name?"

"The older Indians told me that French missionaries had put up a cross on an island." He pointed ahead. "In fact there's Cross Island now."

Then the sun came out, brightly lighting a small rocky island covered with a few scrubby windblown Norways. Larger islands lay beyond to the north.

"Let's stop and have a look," Belva said, as we drew closer.

We got out of the canoe and climbed the island's tilted slabs of black slate.

"I'll bet that's where the base of the cross stood." Belva pointed to a pile of large stones on the highest prominence of the island.

"Didn't any of your diaries say how the lake got its name?" Harvi asked.

"Huysche is the only one. Here's what he had to say about it."

"From Portage de l'Isle a few miles further brought us to Lac la Croix, a long and broad sheet of water, so named by some Jesuit missionaries many years ago, who erected two large wooden crosses on conspicuous islands at the western end of the lake. The crosses have disappeared but the lake retains the name."

I explained to Harvi that the lake's extensions give it a cross shape, and that it probably received its name in a manner similar to that of another Lac la Croix north of Quebec. In 1672 Father François de Crepieul wrote, "all our journeyings . . . came to an end very fittingly at a lake bearing the name of the Cross, from its having the perfect shape of one. To make it bear that beautiful name for a still better reason, we planted many Crosses in its neighborhood."

"There are other explanations, but Huysche's sounds the best to me," Belva declared, as we shoved off to follow the bend of the lake south.

A short paddle brought us opposite Wilkins Bay, where the longest portage on the Dawson Road began. The portage was built to avoid the three Portages la Croix and the Loon River. It led four miles, uphill over ridges and down through swamp, to Sand Point Lake.

Peter O'Leary wrote in his diary after crossing it: "After a very agreeable run [across Lac la Croix towed by a tug] we landed on Nequiquion portage [Dawson portage], the largest of all the portages we travelled over, the length being four miles. Some of the road was very rough, and more of it through swamp, but everywhere along the route traces of

SIR GARNET WOLSELEY'S EXPEDITION

to the Red River in 1869 . . . After a tramp of four miles over the portage, our goods having been sent in a van [cart], we embarked in a large boat, as usual towed by a miniature tug, to cross Lake Nemecan [Namakan Lake]."

We continued to the first Portage de la Croix, Beatty portage. Feeling happy, we sang the favorite rose song of the voyageurs, "J'ai cuelli la belle rose."

> I have cull'd that lovely rosebud,
> I have cull'd that lovely rosebud
> > Hanging on the white rose-plant,
> > > That lovely rosebud,
> > Hanging on the white rose-plant,
> > That lovely rose from white rose plant.

To the voyageurs the water traversed from the first Portage de la Croix, through Loon Lake and Loon River, was known as the Rivière la Croix.

The first portage, now a marine railway 143 yards long, rises gently over a granite outcrop and down into the north arm of Loon Lake. The water from Lac la Croix spills over into Loon Lake only in very high water.

As I looked at the few oaks left on the portage, I realized how homesick Nicholas Garry must have been as he looked at them. Sitting on the portage path in his purple waistcoat, high-collared shirt, tight pants, and leather boots, he wrote, while his voyageurs carried the canoe over:

". . . At ½ past eleven we arrived at the first Portage of La Croix which is about 250 Paces over a Rock covered with Trees. A beautiful Oak on the Banks of the Water brought to my mind England and all I love, all my Friends and Companions. The Sight of Oak never fails to produce this Effect and has the same Influence on the Feelings which the meeting with a Countryman in a distant Clime has on the Spirits."

As we sat resting at the end of the portage before starting on Loon Lake, Harvi asked, "What kind of furs did the old traders take out of the country, and how much were they worth?"

I looked up a note listing the wealth in furs taken out of the Northwest by the French and the North West Company.

Mackenzie listed in 1798:

"The produce . . . consisted of the following furs and peltries:

106,000 Beaver skins,	6000 Lynx skins,
2100 Bear skins,	600 Wolverine skins,
1500 Fox skins,	1650 Fisher skins,
4000 Kitt Fox skins,	100 Rackoon skins,
4600 Otter skins,	3800 Wolf skins,
17,000 Musquash [Muskrat] skins,	700 Elk skins,
32,000 Marten skins,	750 Deer skins,
1800 Mink skins,	1200 Deer skins, dressed,

500 Buffalo robes, and a quantity of castorum.

Using one pound sterling as equal to twenty-four Canadian livres and the pound sterling in turn as very roughly equivalent to five dollars, I read Harvi a few more figures.

During the French regime, in 1717 — 146,395 Canadian livres or about $30,495, in 1755 — 148, 998 livres or $31,040 worth of furs were brought out of the *pays d'en haut.*

The North West Company packed out this total wealth in furs from their various trading departments: 1784–1786, £30,000; 1788, 40,000;

1789, 53,000; 1790–1795, 72,000; 1796–1799, 98,000; and 1800–1804, 107,000. A total of well over $7,710,000!

Harvi shook his head. "Quite an operation."

We headed west in Loon Lake toward the second Portage de la Croix, or Mud portage, which no longer exists, but because of lower water in earlier times, was passed about a half mile before the third Portage de la Croix, today's Loon portage, also a marine railroad. It follows for 228 yards along a series of cascades and lifts over a ridge, down to Loon River.

"Wonder how Loon got its name?" Harvi asked, as he surveyed the streamers of mist rising from the pines on the hilly shores of the lake.

"For loons," I guessed. "The voyageurs referred to it only as part of the Rivière la Croix. But the Indians called it *Un-de-go-sa*, meaning Maneaters Lake."

"Why Maneaters Lake?" Harvi asked.

"There were Indians here who ate human flesh," I explained. "Huysche was one of the diarists who commented on them."

"On one of the portages on Loon Lake we came across some Indians, three old women and some children. One of the old women was the most hideous old hag that it is possible to imagine, skinny, wrinkled, withered, bent, clothed in rags and tatters, and very old. Mr. Pither [Indian agent at Fort Frances] informed us that she was a *cannibal*; that is to say, she had been one of a party some winters previously who had been starved into eating human flesh. We gave these poor creatures a little flour and biscuit, which made them quite happy and contented, and the old hag went up and begged from the men the water in which their pork had been boiled. One of our party that morning was a lady (the only one that accompanied the expedition), who had bravely followed her husband and shared his canoe through all the perils and fatigues of the journey [Frances Ann Hopkins, artist wife of Edward Hopkins, private secretary to Sir George Simpson]. The old hag seemed lost in wonder at the sight of this lady, and truly the contrast between the two was so wonderful, that it was hard to believe that they could be beings of the same nature, hard to realize that the difference between them was only owing to the human agency of education and civilization. The old hag was such a horrid object to look at that we were glad to make our escape from her."

"Speaking of old hags —," Belva began wryly, pushing her hair back and inspecting her fingernails.

I grinned. "If you're looking for a compliment, you're not going to get it."

As we neared Loon portage a vagrant whirl of wind swept out of the woods and flurried down the little strait, scattering ripples in all directions.

Belva grabbed at her hat, then breathed deeply. "Mm, smell," she said. The truant breeze carried the tangy fragrance of the fresh-washed forest — a subtle blend of damp moss, humus, wet bark, and pine, balsam, and cedar.

"I love this spot," Belva said, as we drew near the dock.

Today's portage is on the United States side, but we used the voyageurs' portage on the Canadian side, which begins in a stand of tall white pine. It follows the river which pours down over a bed of rock in a series of drops, the water roaring and churning into white froth at each successive step.

Picking up our packs, we walked through a forest of hoary old Norways and white pine. Soft shafts of light filtered through the arched branches overhead as we walked over copper needles, gold leaves, and bronze bracken.

On the way over the portage, Belva's favorite, she stopped to embrace a Norway, her arms reaching only halfway around.

"I think Grant's description of his camp here is beautiful. May I hear it again?"

When we reached the end of the portage, I read it for her:

". . . the sun having at last come out and this being the best place for pitching tents and the freest from mosquitoes. Tired enough all hands were, and ready for sleep, for these portages are killing work. After taking a swim, we rigged lines before huge fires, and hung up our wet things to dry, so that it was eleven o'clock before anyone could lie down. . . . Our camping ground had been selected by the Indians with their usual good taste. A rocky eminence, round two sides of which a river poured in a roaring linn; on the hill sombre pines, underneath which the tents were pitched; and lower down a forest of white birch. More than one of the party dreamed that he was in Scotland."

150

As we stepped from the shade to the water's edge, the sun brightened to work its autumn alchemy. The leaden day changed to one of gold. Now the snow was gone and the air grew warmer. We took off our parkas, lazily packed the canoe, and started down Loon River.

The stiff semaphore flags of the water reeds pointed the way. The churning wake of a determined flock of mergansers guided us, as they paddled furiously with wings and feet to stay ahead. We followed them downstream past shores of willow and maple and oak, through floating rafts of flame and gold leaves.

Our canoe barely skimmed over the rock outcrop in "56" rapids (numbered from an early logging camp located there). Below the rapids a muskrat swam toward us, brandishing a leaved aspen branch over his head. Seeing us, he turned in dismay and swam headlong into an upended snarl of tree roots. We watched him disentangle himself and then retreat in disgust under an overhanging alder bush.

On we went around points of marsh grass and bulrushes, past little creeks and bays, through beds of bronze lily pads, slipping by sun-drunk turtles lazing on windfalls in the water. As we entered the Mudflats, the mergansers, satisfied with their job of piloting, took to the air over our heads and flew back up the river.

The direct rays of the noon sun intensified the amber hue of the water in the Mudflats. Now the lakes and streams would change in color from those we had passed so far. Draining muskeg and swamp, these waters carry with them dissolved organic matter, especially tannin.

We crossed Little Vermilion Lake to Sand Point Lake.

"Let's stop for lunch on one of those little islands," Belva said, as we started out into Sand Point. "As often as I've been here, I've never visited one."

We headed for the largest of the rocky islands. It was occupied by a haughty seagull who obviously resented our intrusion. As we pulled our canoe up on shore, he flounced off into the water, screaming profanities at us. We spread our lunch under a dwarfed pine that leaned arthritically and clutched with twisted roots at the barren rock. Then we settled down in solid comfort to enjoy our meal of cheese and hardtack.

Harvi looked toward the narrow opening south of the entrance of Loon

River into Sand Point. "Shall we go home?" The narrow opening leads into King William's Narrows between high rock walls to Crane Lake.

"Spoilsport," Belva chided. "We *have* to finish the trip to Rainy."

"You *are* kidding, aren't you, Harvi?" I said. "We're following the Grand Portage route to Rainy Lake, not the Fond du Lac–Vermilion–Crane Lake route. And we *should* finish."

"Is that another old route?" Harvi asked.

"Yes, it's the third route west from Lake Superior. Remember, the Canadians wanted it for the boundary line."

This third route, used by Indians and fur traders to get from Lake Superior to the Northwest, joined the Kaministikwia and Grand Portage "roads" here at Sand Point Lake. Starting at Fond du Lac on Lake Superior, it led up the St. Louis River to Vermilion Lake and down the Vermilion River to Crane Lake.

The Vermilion River roars through a precipitous rock-walled chasm at the gorge, and winds quietly for a mile or so into Crane Lake. The pine-covered shores of this comparatively small lake vary from massive cliffs and ridges to gentle slopes, cut by bays, rivers, and sand beaches. It was known to the Chippewa as *Shuh-shuh-ga Saga-ai-gon* — Blue Heron or Crane Lake — because of the large numbers of herons found there. They raised their young in precariously placed stick nests high in the trees in Northwest Bay. The voyageurs' course through the lake led past Big Bare Island. Then it went between Indian Island and a sand beach, which the Indians used for centuries as a campground. From here it continued north through the Narrows to join the other two waterways at Sand Point. The old traders called Sand Point Lake Vermilion Lake, and considered today's Little Vermilion and Crane Lakes as bays of this one large lake.

While we relaxed in the warm fall sun, I went on to tell Harvi a little of Crane Lake's past.

The first note I read was a description written by Joseph Norwood, a geologist who went through in 1849.

"At Crane Lake Portage [gorge] we found a high ridge of rocks, almost bare . . . The ridge is about three hundred feet in height, and bears east-northeast and west-southwest. . . .

"The rapids here are very difficult, and a portage has to be made of

152

everything. Where the river turns round, or, rather, cuts through the ridge just described, it is contracted to twenty feet in width, and runs through a gorge, with mural walls over forty feet in height, for the distance of nearly three hundred yards. From the point where the portage leaves the river above the ridge, to where it strikes it again, on the north side, is about a mile and a half by the course of the stream — the length of the portage being estimated by the voyageurs at two "pauses" [*posés*]. The fall at these rapids . . . is thirty five feet.

"A little over two miles below the portage we entered a narrow *detroit*, which leads to Crane Lake. The shores of the lake are bound with rocks, which become more granitic in character, and just at the termination of the lake, low ridges of granite show themselves. . . . The bendings and foldings of the slate by the granitic intrusions, are beautifully exhibited at many points on the lake shore, and particularly at the narrow strait [King William's Narrows] which connects Crane Lake with Sand Points Lake, and called by the Indians Wa-bá-bi-kon [white clay]. . . .

"I neglected to say, in the proper place, that from representations made regarding the difficulty of finding our way . . . we procured a guide at Crane Portage, from a company of men in the service of the Hudson's Bay Company, who were encamped there for the purpose of trading with the Indians."

At the foot of the gorge, where the Hudson's Bay camp was located, the water rushes down into a pool covered with white foam. The margins of the pool are formed, on the east, by a high ridge covered with jackpine and on the west, by a point of land, a favorite campsite of Indians in ages past. On this point, securely protected from winter winds and on the Indian waterway, are rectangular mounds now grown over with brush which give evidence that men occupied with the fur trade once lived here.

On this same point Bourassa, one of La Vérendrye's voyageurs, built a fort in 1736. An entry in La Vérendrye's diary described the event.

"Dec. 1736. On the 22 Dec. six canoes arrived light from Michilimackinac with 29 men. They told me that they had left at Vermillion River [Crane Portage] the small quantity of merchandise which they had brought up, and that Bourassa and Eustache were remaining in charge of it with 12 men, their intention being to winter there to the injury of Fort St. Pierre

153

[Pither's Point, Rainy Lake] and to trade with the Sauteur [Chippewa] This river is on the route taken by our enemies [the Sioux]. I immediately dispatched a savage to whom I gave 40 beaver skins to carry orders to them to go at once to Fort St. Pierre and to forbid them to winter at Vermillion River. On the 22 three Frenchmen arrived from Vermillion River bringing me letters from Bourassa and Eustache in which they excused themselves for not having executed my orders on the ground that they had only received them on All Saints' Day. They inform me that a great number of Salteur [Chippewa] have sought refuge with them through fear of the Sioux. They questioned them closely in order to ascertain how the Frenchmen [La Vérendrye's son, Jean Baptiste, Father Aulneau, and eighteen voyageurs had been massacred on an island in the Lake of the Woods] had been killed, but they were unwilling to say, though amongst them there was one Salteur who had been present at the tragedy. On the 27th the Sieur Dovere, one of the clerks of the company, having asked to be allowed to go with six men to Vermillion River, I granted him permission and entrusted him with a letter in which I instructed Bourassa and Eustache to construct a little fort around the two houses so as to be less exposed to attack, and in the early spring to send goods to Fort St. Pierre to exchange with the savages who are accustomed to resort thither, and also to repair to the fort."

Many years later, undoubtedly at this same location, the North West Company maintained a wintering post. Its occupant for several trading seasons between 1806 and 1821 was Dr. John McLoughlin.

After receiving his license to practice medicine in 1803, young Mc-Loughlin left his home in Rivière du Loup, Canada, for the *pays d'en haut*, to become a clerk and surgeon for the North West Company. He was a large man with piercing eyes that soon saw the beauty of the autumn color and winter storms on Crane Lake, where he traded with the Indians. While here, his half-breed wife, Marguerite Wadin, bore his children, Eloisa, Eliza, and John. When not engaged in trading, the kind "Big Doctor," Minnesota's first, frequently treated ailing Indians and sick voyageurs. So well did he come to know the Minnesota-Ontario boundary country that he was placed in charge of the Lac la Pluie district of the North West Company in 1814.

154

Seven years later, when the Hudson's Bay Company absorbed the Nor'Westers, McLoughlin left for Oregon country as chief factor for the Columbia district of the Hudson's Bay Company. Over the years that followed, the "White Headed Eagle," as he came to be known, abandoned the cause of the fur trade for that of civilization. His activities to aid American settlers in the Oregon territory earned him fame after his death and the title "Father of Oregon."

After union, the Hudson's Bay Company had taken over all the North West Company's establishments. On Crane Lake they met and successfully overcame unexpected competition. In 1822, George Johnston, a petty trader from Sault Ste. Marie, had concentrated his main strength of ten men at his Crane Lake post. In an abortive attempt to take the buildings of the Hudson's Bay Company by force, with so few men and but limited resources, he was naturally unsuccessful, and the Hudson's Bay Company continued operations after driving him from the area.

When I had finished telling all this to Harvi, we pushed on through Pointe de Sable — Sand Point, where Alexander Henry the younger in 1800 "found some Indians making canoes." We passed Burnt Island and the numerous small islands guarding the entrance to Namakan Narrows.

Two thirds of the way through the narrows, on the Canadian side, is a cliff of mica slate. Just above the present water level is a long serpentine fold of flesh-colored feldspar, which the Indians worshiped as a water manitou. Near the manitou are reddish-brown pictographs of moose, men in canoes, a large headless animal, a small cat-like animal, a pipe, a manitou, suns, and footprints. Oddly enough two of these figures, a moose and a mark resembling the Venus's mirror symbol, are in white pigment. So far no other white pictographs have been found in the Quetico-Superior. Of this white pigment Delafield wrote "Below the Manitou Rapid [on Rainy River] is found the white earth, which is used as a pigment by the Indians & by the Canadians mixed with sturgeon oil."

A few years ago we noticed that a slab, containing some of these pictographs, had broken away from the main mass, and was about to fall into the water, where it would have been irretrievably lost. To prevent this we removed it and later presented it to the Canadian government. The slab with its pictographs is now on display in the Royal Museum in Toronto.

155

Joseph Norwood was the first to observe the paintings, in 1849. "At a point, called by the Indians Wa-bi-se-gon, near the entrance to Nemakan or Sturgeon Lake, is an exposure of mica slate, with felspar veins, . . . which, from the resemblance of one of the veins to a serpent, is regarded by the Indians as a *manitou* or god, and must be highly esteemed by them, from the quantity of vermilion bestowed on it, and the number of animals depicted on the face of the rock."

We left the Painted Rocks and the narrows to enter Namakan Lake.

The Chippewa called the lake Nah-ma or Sturgeon. In those early days, as well as now, these archaic boneless fishes abounded in the waters of the lake. Mackenzie noted that the lake was named "from a particular place at the foot of a fall [Kettle Falls], where the natives spear sturgeon."

From the time of the Nor'Westers the way through the lake was five miles west-northwest to Bare or Soldiers' portage, first Petit Portage Neuf, which was "the safest and shortest" way to Rainy Lake.

As we emerged from the narrows we could see the wide expanse of Namakan between two of the many islands scattered at the east end of the lake. The water was tranquil. Beyond the reef Gull Island floated, chalky white, like a mirage in the distance. We felt fortunate that a strong wind wasn't blowing from the west; for when it does, not even the most foolhardy canoeist would dare venture on the white-capped fury that is Namakan.

We turned northeast and, passing behind the islands, followed the eastern shore of the lake. The islands are mostly tilted slabs of granite, leaning steeply to the south. Some green with pine and cedar, others just barren rock, they lay like so many listing ships in the water. Often we had visited the little hidden coves on these islands to pick up satiny driftwood bleaching on the honey-colored sand of the beaches.

We came to the mouth of Namakan River, which begins on the north shore of Lac la Croix, then curves westward to end in Namakan Lake. It is a most treacherous river, filled with canoe-shattering rapids, falls, and swift currents. It was not commonly traveled by fur traders, but was used for awhile when it was considered a part of the boundary line. Projecting from the west shore of the river, at its mouth, is Tar Point, a level spot with a grove of oaks and elms, used for centuries as a campsite by the In-

156

dians, who had a sturgeon fishery just off its shores. We drifted in the canoe, looking at the point and thinking about its past.

"The first time I came down the river I felt like Lady Simpson," Belva declared. "Only it was more terrifying for me as a bowswoman — I didn't have a steersman manning the canoe, and the river was filled with logs."

"No sarcasm," I countered. "I didn't cut my teeth on a paddle like you did."

"Don't feel too bad. I'd call you half a voyageur now." She settled herself comfortably in the canoe. "Why don't you read some of the things Lady Simpson and the others wrote as they went down the river?"

So I opened the pack and, finding the notes, read from Lady Simpson's diary. "descended the river Michan [Namakan] which is not the usual route, but much shorter; yet seldom or never passed by Whites, being considered dangerous. The other route is understood to be within the American territory, and this, to be the line of demarkation: being the great outlet of the Waters running from the height of land thro' Lac and Riviere la Pluie, into Lac des Bois [Lake of the Woods]. Mr. Simpson therefore in order to ascertain its state, mounted its current last Fall, in low water, and descended it this Season in high water, and considers it not only a practicable, but a safe route in any state, either for Boats or Canoes.

"We made 3 Portages, and ran several Rapids, which before entering had rather an alarming appearance; but once over the brink, the rapidity with which they were passed, left no time for apprehension; on the contrary, I could but admire the address of the Bowsman in leading our beautiful & airy bark, thro' the Breakers, Whirlpools, & Eddies occasioned by this great body of water pent up between immense walls of Rock, and hurled over huge masses of the same material.

"The river we had been descending, empties itself into a beautiful Lake of the same name; where we fell in with a large Camp of Indians attending a Sturgeon Fishery [Tar Point]: they received us with a salute of fire-arms, and we replied to them by a present of Tobacco, which seemed to afford great satisfaction."

"Even then Tar Point was a favorite spot for sturgeon fishing," Belva commented, "and it still is. Let's hear Hind's experience now."

"In descending the Grand Rapids [Lady Rapids], my canoe had a nar-

157

row escape. Lambert acted as steersman, and Charley, an Ojibway Indian, as bow-man. Lambert was not strong enough to give the proper direction to the canoe in order to avoid a rock jutting out at the head of the rapid. Just as we made the leap, the stern, borne swiftly round by the current, grazed the rock and tore the bark, without, however, doing serious damage. The moment Charley felt the graze, he turned round, brandished his paddle, and shook it at the unfortunate Lambert; we shot down the rapid with great velocity, and embraced the opportunity afforded by the first safe eddy to examine the bark of the canoe. We were deeply laden, and the bottom of the canoe was so covered with our baggage, that no part was visible. 'Put your fingers to the bottom of the canoe, monsieur,' said Lambert to me; 'how much water?' 'Two inches,' I replied. 'That will do, we shall not make more water now we are out of the rapid, it is only a crack, and the bark is tough.' We made, however, three inches of water in a short time, and as the baggage was in danger of being wetted, it was deemed advisable to gum the leak without unnecessary delay."

Belva and I just glanced at each other and smiled, for on our trip she had brandished the paddle at me a few times too!

I read Bigsby next.

"We ascended it [Namakan River] on our return home, entering from a small, quiet bay in Lake Namaycan, full of reeds and water-lilies, its shores lined with long grass and fine young oaks: but when once in the river all is romantic — that is, beautiful and dangerous.

"This stream is a chain of vehement rapids and still waters; the former pent up in high walls of black basalt, from thirty to sixty yards apart, and crowned with pines; the latter, wide, full of marshy islets, rushes, and lilies. It is twelve or fifteen miles long — more, perhaps — and leaves Lake Lacroix by a series of pretty cascades and rapids.

"Two miles up the river from Namaycan [Lady Rapids] the rapids were hardly practicable. We therefore unloaded, and scrambled over the tangled cliffs for a considerable distance, using the tow-rope to the canoes. But good and new as the tow-rope was, the strain was too great; it broke, and away went the first canoe down the heaving, foaming rapid, ten miles an hour, our two men in her escaping by miracle almost.

"Just as a bend of the river took our distressed people out of sight,

158

looking up the stream, we saw a long spear erect in the water, and riding rapidly toward us. This I could not at all understand; but in a moment or two there darted down the current, from an upper bend, a canoe in full pursuit, one Indian at the bow, standing aloft on the thwarts, spear in hand; another was guiding. In striking a large fish, it had wrenched the weapon from the hand of the spearsman.

"The river is unfit for commercial purposes, a fact we had to verify, because other formidable rapids, as well as cascades, are met with beside this. The falls near Lake Lacroix are pleasing [Snake Falls].

"We slept on the lake-shore, just above the portage, and had to complain of the singular cry of the whip-poor-will all night, in a tree close to us, screaming into our ears his unhappy, reproachful notes, without a moment's cessation. . . .

"In a wood close by, which had lately been fired, I found a beautiful tomahawk-hatchet. I took it in return for many little valuables left behind in our twilight morning starts."

I had a couple of other comments about Tar Point. One was Graham's, who in 1847 passed through the "eternal pine forests," down the Namakan River "with a running accompaniment of frogs and crickets from the shore" and through rapids guided by old Batiste, "the old fellow as cool all the time as if eating his dinner," and on to Tar Point, "the Indians' sturgeon-fishing water.

"Towards evening we passed a large Saulteux village encamped there for sturgeon, and it was a curious sight, situated on a cleared spot at a beautiful bend of the river. I took their bark lodges at first for a fort, but was soon undeceived, as, the moment the canoe song was heard, a hundred whooping savages rushed to their canoes, and were dashing round us in all directions, like so many dolphins. Very fine, clean-made fellows, naked as Adam, and their faces painted all the colours of the rainbow. As I sat up in the canoe, to look at the sight, I had to do all the hand-shaking of the party, which was not a remarkably agreeable task."

The other comment was one of Palliser's, made in 1857. "We halted on the right bank of the river at one of the most lovely spots for agricultural purposes that we have seen on the whole route. There was something in the natural grouping of the trees and shrubs at this place which irresistibly

159

called to mind rural scenes at home, and it was hard to realize the fact that the hand of man had taken no part in producing this effect. We found here the remains of an Indian camp, among which, in a secluded grove, were several coffins raised above the ground upon posts to the height of 5 or 6 feet."

After reading the notes we crossed Namakan Lake along its north shore to Bare portage. On the way we wondered where David Thompson, on a Sunday in 1797, "went to 2 Tents of Sotees about 6 men — They had killed a Moose. The men traded about 10 lbs of fresh Meat from them for corn."

Somewhere on the lake he had also held Sunday services. What a picture he must have made: a short man, with darkened skin and square-cut hair, a Protestant reading his Bible to a group of intent Roman Catholic voyageurs "in most extraordinarily pronounced French, three chapters out of the Old Testament, and as many out of the New, adding such explanations as seemed to him suitable" (Bigsby).

We camped at the portage for the night. Here was our journey's end through the Quetico-Superior. According to Hind we had portaged 15.33 miles over thirty-two carrying places and covered a total distance of 207.86 miles from Lake Superior to Rainy Lake. Our course over the old Grand Portage route, with minor variations, was identical with the present international boundary which, in turn, follows and, in fact, was determined by the route of the voyageurs. While only a short section of the way from Montreal to the Northwest, it was a most important part of the explorers' and traders' road. Equally important to us, it remains much the same as when the songs of the voyageurs echoed from its shores of pine and rock.

The road from here passed over Bare portage, a brush-covered rocky outcrop, and then led (in Hind's words) "into a narrow circuitous river, without perceptible current, which meanders through a reedy expanse, fringed with low willows for about three miles. The canoe route then takes a winding course, whose general direction is nearly due north for a distance of two and a half miles, when turning westward we suddenly arrive at the open and beautiful, but indescribably barren and desolate region of Rainy Lake."

Rainy Lake is the largest body of water traversed after Grand Portage.

160

Known originally as Tekamamiouen, it later became Lac la Pluie, from the rainlike mist over the falls at the outlet of the lake.

The course from Hale Bay wound through numerous straits to the outlet of the lake and Rainy River. The river began with two rapids at Pither's Point, and then, after a mile and a third, poured over three ridges in a twenty foot drop into a roaring torrent. This Chute de la Chaudière necessitated a portage of one hundred and fifty yards on the Canadian side, Portage de la Chaudière, which began at the foot of what is Portage Street in Fort Frances.

One or more posts occupied the area about the falls almost continuously from 1688, when de Noyon built the first French post, to 1902, when the last Hudson's Bay Company post burned down. La Vérendrye's Fort St. Pierre stood on Pither's Point. The North West Company had a fort on a high bank one mile below the falls on the Canadian side from about 1780 to 1821. The first Hudson's Bay Company's establishment was located from 1792 to 1798 below that of the North West Company. The later Hudson's Bay post, which stood from 1816 to 1902, was built just below the falls in a little bay on the Canadian side. The American Fur Company fort stood directly opposite on the American side from 1822 to 1833.

From these forts the "road" continued down the Rainy River to Lake of the Woods and then through the Winnipeg River to Lake Winnipeg. At Lake Winnipeg the traders could follow routes to every part of the continent — to Hudson Bay, to the Minnesota and Mississippi, to the Missouri, through the Rockies and Columbian waters to the Pacific, and from Athabaskan waters and the Mackenzie River all the way to the Arctic Ocean.

While staking the tent I paused to glance upward in one of those instants of intense awareness that happen in the wilderness. It was a moment of stillness when the forest stood in hushed anticipation. Then I felt the peace that is the golden benediction of day's end in this enchanted land. In this sanctuary of pines and water, not even the cynic can remain untouched by the beauty of a sunset.

The sun hovered in its descent, its glow reflected in the incandescence of the clouds. When it dropped from sight, the clouds blazed red, then subsided in a radiant flush of rose. The lake glistened in reflected glory

161

and the forest was bathed in a champagne haze that erupted over the pines in a halo of flame.

In the green-gold afterglow a chipmunk, startled when Harvi broke some sticks for the fire, sputtered hurriedly over the rocks. I turned reluctantly to finish my task.

Choosing this last night's menu was no problem. The food pack was nearly empty. As I picked up the pack, I was puzzled by its weight and set it down to investigate. Rocks! Exactly eighteen pounds, I found out later. Belva was watching me. She didn't wait for questions.

"Now, look, I was carrying them in the duffel. The food pack looked pretty empty when we stopped for lunch, so I just transferred them. That's all. Don't you dare — !"

I was hefting one in my hand. She thought I was going to throw it away, but I didn't have the heart. After carrying them herself all this distance, she deserved to keep them. I dumped them out to see what she had — banded agates from Moose Lake, Height of Land, and Swamp portage, rose quartz from Upper Basswood Falls, travertine from Prairie portage, jasper and flint from Gunflint, and rock crystal from Namakan. She watched me with a look of relief as I put them back.

When we had finished the supper dishes, Harvi volunteered, "I'll read tonight." We had read Bigsby at Tar Point, so I handed him the notes from Delafield. He leaned against a rock, crossed his legs, pushed his hat back, and began to read. "Arrive at the Lac l'Croix Portage about 10 a.m. It is a short post, and leads to a small lake, of 6 miles length, that my guide says is called Un-de-go-sa, or Man-eaters Lake; but it is more properly perhaps the l'Croix River. It leads to another portage, called the Second l'Croix Portage. It contains several little rocky islands & there is not much, if any current. A crooked creek connects the Second with the Third l'Croix Portage, a very short and easy post, from whence we follow the l'Croix River 5 or 6 miles into Vermillion Lake. It is a narrow, winding stream of gentle current, with low and marshy shores, about 50 feet wide. When passing the several l'Croix Portages, met ten canoes, laden with packs from the interior for Fort William. It was a wholesome lesson for my men to witness the industry, activity, & labor of these crews on the portages. It was the best conducted strife (for it was a race) that under the circumstances I can

162

imagine. Several arriving at the same moment at a landing only large enough to admit them by studied contrivances, all unlade, carry their packs, their canoes, load again and are off, without a word being exchanged. The portage was made upon the trot in every instance. Of three canoes that went thro' these routines whilst I was present, I did not hear a word spoken. Before I had made the portage another brigade came up, who were nearly as intent as the first. Soon after I passed the third detachment, and as they had no hope of regaining their lost ground, they travelled with less speed. This brigade was following the trader, Mr. Nelson, whom I pass'd on Lac l'Croix.

"Leaving the l'Croix River enter upon Vermillion Lake. It is a small lake of 7 or 8 miles length with several islands. They are of granite, having gentle inclinations to the lake. No highlands in sight. From Vermillion Lake pass thro' a narrows formed of granite rocks into Lake Nemecan. The change of country is now almost as remarkable as the change of occurrences. The precipitous cliffs & lofty mountain ranges of the Old Road have disappeared. The country is still all rock, but the rocks are not very high & are generally sloping & covered with wood. The meeting of fellow travellers & the bustle & activity of the crews of laden canoes, who seem to be driving the most arduous of all trades, gives the scene a still more striking contrast. On the Old Road from Lake Superior to Lac l'Croix I did not meet a single traveller of any description, and accidentally with two small parties of Indians. The entrance into Lake Nemecan was made pleasant by a soft and bright afternoon and a calm lake. Islands as usual in all directions obstructed the view, and generally confine it to a mile or so in extent. Several Indians from their wigwams on the islands, aroused by the chant of my light hearted crew, give chase in their little canoes. I was unwilling to be delayed by them, and being desirous to improve a delightful evening, encamp beyond their reach. I found however, that they would follow me, so that I allowed them to come up. They brought presents of blueberries, that grow in this country in very great profusion and large, for which I give them some tobacco and leave them. One of the men had a collar on his neck curiously ornamented with claws of animals that I wanted to buy, but he said he liked it too much to part with it. After proceeding a mile or more, I perceived one of the canoes in chase again &

163

anxious to encamp beyond their sight or knowledge, stop'd for him. He proved to be a young Indian dispatched with a collar for me, ornamented with claws. He said that they feared I would take them for bad Indians because I did not get the collar, but they were good Indians; that they thought my unwillingness to stop was because they were bad Indians, but they were good Indians. I gave him tobacco & a glass of whiskey which he ask'd for, saying it would make him very happy, for the collar, and assured him that I thought them good Indians. He left us much pleased with his errand and his bargain.

"My crew seemed elated by the splendor of the evening; a rising moon and perfectly placid lake render the travelling agreeable and I proceed for 8 miles beyond the Indians and encamp in a good place on an island. The men ask'd if I would go on, but believing that they would take as much time from the following day, to cook &c. I thought it more advisable to stop. Of the distance travelled in the course of a day, I make no mention, partly because any estimate of mine, made of a route thro' islands and over portages &c., in a canoe, the rate of going of which I know not, would be very uncertain; and because when our surveys are complete, they can be ascertained with precision.

"Descent of the three Lac l'Croix portages is about 44 feet. . . .

"Saturday, July 26. Having made a good day's journey yesterday over two lakes and part of two others, over three portages and the connecting straits, I give the men time to clean themselves & have breakfast, and the usual gumming of the canoe being done, embark on Nemecan Lac at 7 a.m. Sturgeon and whitefish abound in this handsome lake and the Indians resort here occasionally to take them. It continues choked with islands, mostly small. When speaking of islands in this country, the explanation should be made that small and large rocks, or ranges of rocks, are always meant. The decay of leaves &c., in the crevices encourages the growth of the small pine, birch and cedar that cover such as have crevices or uneven surfaces. If smooth, they are bare of vegetation of any kind. The soil or earth however begins to increase, and at the portages and in the vallies I have seen several places where I could drive a tent pin! The islands of Lake Nemecan are of granite and micaceous schist (I think), both alternating and associating. Veins of white quartz run thro' the mica rock, sometimes winding like serpents in form. The micaceous rock is usually at an inclination of near 45° to the N. still running E. and W., & a little N. of E. & S. of W. The granite now contains a fair proportion of mica, and the hornblend is disappearing in the granite, and is remarkable for the large masses of flesh color'd feldspar and white quartz that it contains quite distinct from each other. Leave Lake Nemecan over a short portage into a narrow, winding strait half a mile long, that carries us to another short portage, from whence we pass into another narrow, winding strait about 3 miles long into Lac l'Pluie. The first of these is called the Little New Portage of Lac Nemecan. There is another and more direct water communication from Lac Nemecan to Lac l'Pluie by the Nemecan River, which is S. of the Little New Portage, & where the Line will pass. It is said to be a longer route & therefore not travelled. One short portage only is to be made, which is over the Chaudière Falls of the River Nemecan, and they empty directly into Lac l'Pluie. There are no rapids in the River Nemecan, so that there can be nothing but the choice of a shorter road with two portages, that gives the route I pass'd an advantage over the longer one with one portage, in the estimation of the canoe men. The Chaudière Falls are so called because of a hole worn in the rock at the side of the fall in shape like a kettle, which the tradition is, was the work of savages. It is plainly the work of a boulder stone set in motion by the rapids when they overflowed the spot, of which fact there are ample other evidences. The little stream by which I descended to Lac l'Pluie has a gentle current, is of 20 & 30 yards width, and winds the greater part of its distance thro' rushes and high grass."

Harvi finished reading and handed me the notes.

We sat longer around the campfire on this final night. A little nostalgic already, we talked of the singing rapids, the silent portage paths, our campsites, the long reaches of the lakes and their many moods. From now on, they would be inextricably woven with our portage into the past.

The coals of our fire flared once more in the slight evening breeze. Out of the mists creeping over the lake, a loon called and then it was quiet.

ACKNOWLEDGMENTS

Note of appreciation

I owe a special debt to two people whose talents have enhanced everyone's enjoyment of the Quetico-Superior country. To have had the enthusiastic encouragement and guidance of such an accomplished writer as Florence Page Jaques was an inspiration, and to have the exquisite artistry of Francis Lee Jaques illustrate the book is a privilege indeed. Their support was a most gratifying experience; I can only hope they know my appreciation.

Anyone who probes into the history of the Minnesota-Ontario boundary region owes more than can be repaid to Grace Lee Nute's exhaustive research, which has made material available that might otherwise still remain in obscurity.

I should like to thank those members of the staff of the Minnesota Historical Society who gave kind assistance during the preparation of the manuscript; William Trygg for information about the location of trading posts on Basswood Lake; Mary Nakasone for preparing the maps; and my daughter, Gretchen, for transcribing passages from the diaries.

For permission to reproduce passages, I give sincere acknowledgment to the following persons and organizations:

The Hudson's Bay Company for the passages from the appendix to the seventeenth volume of the Hudson's Bay Record Society's publications (*Moose Fort Journals 1783–85*).

The Champlain Society for the excerpts from W. Stewart Wallace, *Documents Relating to the North West Company*, and Lawrence J. Burpee, *Journals and Letters of La Vérendrye and his Sons*.

Major General John Ross Delafield for portions of his grandfather's diary, *The Unfortified Boundary*, and his thoughtfulness in sending me a copy of the original diary.

Mrs. G. H. Haddon, a great-granddaughter of Sir George Simpson, for quotations from Lady Frances Simpson's diary, which she owns.

Northwestern University Press for use of portions of Kennicott's diary in *The First Scientific Exploration of Russian America and the Purchase of Alaska*.

J. A. B.

BIBLIOGRAPHY AND INDEX

For those who want to learn more

Bigsby, John J. *The Shoe and Canoe.* London: Chapman and Hall, 1850.

Burpee, Lawrence J. *The Search for the Western Sea.* Toronto: Macmillan Company of Canada, Limited, 1935.

———, editor. *Journals and Letters of Pierre Gaultier de Varennes de La Vérendrye and His Sons.* Toronto: Champlain Society, 1927.

Campbell, Marjorie Wilkins. *The North West Company.* New York: St. Martin's Press, 1957.

Coues, Elliott, editor. *New Light on the Early History of the Greater Northwest: The Manuscript Journals of Alexander Henry . . . and of David Thompson . . . 1799–1814 . . .* New York: Harper, 1897. 3 v.

Davidson, Gordon C. *The North West Company.* Berkeley: University of California Press, 1918.

Delafield, Major Joseph. *The Unfortified Boundary.* Edited by Robert McElroy and Thomas Riggs. New York: privately printed, 1943.

Garry, Nicholas. *Diary.* In *Transactions of the Royal Society of Canada,* second series, v. 6, sec. 2, pp. 73–204. Ottawa, 1900.

Gates, Charles M., editor. *Five Fur Traders of the Northwest.* Minneapolis: University of Minnesota Press, 1933.

Graham, Frederick Ulric. *Notes of a Sporting Expedition in the Far West of Canada, 1847.* Edited by Jane Hermione Graham. London, 1898.

Grant, George M. *Ocean to Ocean.* Toronto: Radisson Society of Canada, Limited, 1925.

Harmon, Daniel W. *A Journal of Voyages and Travels in the Interior of North America . . .* Toronto: Courier Press, 1911.

Henry, Alexander. *Travels and Adventures in Canada and the Indian Territories between the Years 1760 and 1776.* Edited by James Bain. Boston: Little, Brown, and Company, 1901.

173

Hind, Henry Y. *Narrative of the Canadian Red River Exploring Expedition of 1857* . . . London: Green, Longman, and Roberts, 1860. 2 v.

Huysche, Guy L. *The Red River Expedition.* London and New York: Macmillan Company, 1871.

Innis, Harold A. *The Fur Trade in Canada.* New Haven: Yale University Press, 1930.

Jacobs, Peter. *Journal of the Reverend Peter Jacobs.* New York, 1857.

James, James Alton. *The First Scientific Exploration of Russian America and the Purchase of Alaska.* Evanston and Chicago: Northwestern University, 1943.

McKay, Douglas. *The Honourable Company.* Indianapolis and New York: Bobbs-Merrill Company, 1936.

Mackenzie, Alexander. *Voyages from Montreal through the Continent of North America to the Frozen and Pacific Oceans in 1789 and 1793* . . . London: R. Noble, 1801.

Nute, Grace Lee. *The Voyageur.* New York: Appleton and Company, 1931.

———. *The Voyageurs' Highway.* St. Paul: Minnesota Historical Society, 1941.

———. *Rainy River Country.* St. Paul: Minnesota Historical Society, 1950.

O'Leary, Peter. *Travels and Experiences in Canada, the Red River Territory and the United States.* London: John B. Day, 1875.

Owen, David Dale. *Report of a Geological Survey of Wisconsin, Iowa, and Minnesota* . . . Philadelphia: Lippincott, Grambo, and Company, 1852.

Rich, E. E. *Hudson's Bay Company.* London: Hudson's Bay Company Record Society, 1958 and 1959. 2 v.

Tanner, John. *A Narrative of the Captivity and Adventures of John Tanner.* Edited by Edwin James. New York: G. & C. & H. Carvill; London: Baldwin & Cradock; Thomas Ward, 1830.

Tyrrell, J. B., editor. *David Thompson's Narrative of His Explorations in Western America, 1784–1812.* Toronto: Champlain Society, 1916.

Index

American Fur Co.: purchase of North West Co. posts, 6; enters border struggle with Hudson's Bay Co., 7; founded, 7; Fond du Lac department, 7; posts in northern Minnesota, 7; agreement with Hudson's Bay Co., 8

American Revolution, 5, 7, 34

Arrow Lake, 73

Askin, John: construction of Grand Portage fort, 42

Astor, John Jacob, 7, 8; founds American Fur Co., 7; persuades Congress to prohibit foreign traders, 7

Athabaska House (Rainy Lake), 39, 124

Athabaska region, 123

Auchagah, 33

Aulneau, Father Jean: quoted, 65–66; 114

Bare portage, 156, 160

Bas de la Rivière (Winnipeg River), 60

Basswood Lake, 4, 6, 8, 22, 99–109

Basswood River, 109–112, 117, 118–119

Beatty portage, 147–148

Beauharnois, Charles, Marquis de: quoted, 75

Belcourt, Rev. Georges Antoine, 132

Bennett, Lieut. Thomas, 42

Big Knife portage, 98

Big Rock portage, 62–63

Bigsby, Dr. John: boundary commissioner, 25; on whiskey jack, 51; on cascades on Pigeon River, 55; on the Meadow, 60; on view from Goose Rock, 64; from Gunflint Lake to Lake Saganaga, 88–91; from Lake Saganaga to Basswood Lake, 103–104; Hudson's Bay Co. post on Basswood Lake, 104; Basswood Lake to Crooked Lake, 118–119; on Picture Rock (Crooked Lake), 114; Iron Lake to Lac la Croix, 126–127; Namakan River, 158–159

Birch Lake, 99

Blanchet, Rev. Francis Norbert, 132

Bois Blanc. *See* Basswood Lake

Bottle Lake, 123

Bottle portage, 123

Bourassa, René, 25; La Vérendrye on, 153–154

Boundary: U.S.-Canada, disputes and settlement, 95

Bourgeois: defined, 40; night encampment, 116

Bustard portage, 63

Canoe factories: Grand Portage, 38;

175

Lake Saganaga, 83; Basswood Lake, 107–108; Sand Point Lake, 155
Canoe, Montreal (canot du maître): description, 38; loading, 43
Canoe, north (canot du nord): description, 56–57; number, 123–124
Caribou portage, 62, 63
Carp portage, 99
Carp Lake, 99
Cascades (Pigeon River): Bigsby on, 55; Owen on, 55–56
Castor gras d'hiver: defined, 21
Charles II, King, 5, 9
Champlain, Samuel de, 30
Coureurs de bois, 23; Washington Irving on, 32
Crepieul, Father François, 147
Corbet, Vincent, 133
Couteaux. See Knife Lake
Crane Lake, 4, 6, 25, 26, 152, 153, 154–155
Crooked Lake, 22, 113–122
Cross Island (Lac la Croix), 146
Curry, Thomas, 34
Curtain Falls (Crooked Lake), 122
Cypress Lake, 96–98

Dawson portage, 147
Dawson Road, 8–10. See also Kaministikwia route
Dawson-Hind expedition, 9
Dawson, Simon, 9, 16, 133
de Noyon, Jacques, 131
Décharge: defined, 62
Degradé: defined, 87
Delafield, Maj. Joseph: boundary commissioner, 25; mode of portaging, 49–50; canoe repair on New Long portage, 77; Gunflint Lake to Lake Saganaga, 91–94; importance to U.S. in boundary dispute, 95; Lake Saganaga to Basswood Lake, 104–106; Hudson's Bay Co. post on Basswood Lake, 106; Basswood Lake to Crooked Lake, 117–118; Picture Rock (Crooked Lake), 114–115; Crooked Lake to Lac la Croix, 127–129; Lac la Croix to Namakan Lake, 162–165
Demers, Rev. Modest, 132

Dérouine: defined, 101
Dickson, Robert, 6
Dumoulin, Rev. Sévère, 132

Eastern border lakes: geology, 64; described, 78
Edge, Rev. William, 132
Engagé: defined, 43
Evans, Rev. James, 125, 133
Exploration: French, 4, 34; British, 45–47 passim

Faries, Hugh: passages from Rainy River post journal, 101–102
Fleming, Sandford, 133
Fond du Lac, 8
Fort Charlotte, 29, 39; described, 54; Delafield on, 54
Fort Frances, 6, 132
Fort Garry (Winnipeg), 7, 9
Fort Gibraltar, 6
Fort Maurepas, 34
Fort St. Pierre, 4, 34, 161
Fort St. Charles: La Vérendrye's headquarters, 34; mentioned, 114
Fort William, 6, 22, 131; rendezvous of North West Co., 80
Fowl portage, 63
Frobisher, Thomas, 34
Fur Trade: French develop basic features, 4; early practices of British, 5; activity in Quetico-Superior country, 8; French struggle with British for use of Hudson's Bay, 30; relation to exploration, 32; trade goods, 37; importance of Athabaska region, 46; interior of posts described, 65; important elements, 76; traders in Quetico-Superior country, 100; importance of Quetico-Superior posts, 100; daily life at posts, 100–103; value of French furs, 148; value of North West Co. furs, 148–149. See also Quetico-Superior country; individual lakes; North West Co.; Hudson's Bay Co.; American Fur Co.

Galette: Kennicott on, 137
Garry, Nicholas, 112–113, 131; quot-

ed, 112, 129; encampment, 116; Beatty portage, 148

Ghent, Treaty of, 25

Goose portage, 63

Goose Rock (South Fowl Lake), 64; Bigsby on, 64

Gorge (Crane Lake): described, 152–154 *passim*; Norwood on, 152–153

Graham, Frederick Ulric, 133; on Namakan River, 159

Grand Portage: after American Revolution, 4; becomes U.S. territory, 4; French post, 4; North West Co. post, 6, 28; American Fur Co. post, 8; mentioned, 8, 22; description, 28–44 *passim*; creek, 28; importance to fur trade, 34; inland depot and rendezvous for North West Co., 34; Macdonell on, 35; Indians, 38; cargo vessels, 39; Nelson on, 40; XY Co. post, 40; Irving on, 40–41; fort rebuilt and dedicated, 42; Mackenzie on, 42; annual ball, 44; Harmon on, 44; abandoned for Fort William, 80

Grand Portage route: mentioned, 4, 131, 160; defined, 22; French explorers and traders, 30, 32; La Vérendrye on, 34; Saint-Pierre on, 45; British explorers and traders, 45–47; weight of trade goods carried over portages, 94–95; boundary dispute, 95; junction with Kaministikwia route, 144–145

Grand Portage trail: mentioned, 22, 29; described, 48–49; significance in history, 49; Mackenzie on, 49, 51–52; *1688* rock, 50; Henry the younger on, 50; Bigsby on, 51

Granite River, 22, 82–83, 88, 92–93

Grant, Rev. George, 10, 133; shooting rapids, 138–139; at Isle portage, 144; Loon portage, 150

Great Cherry portage, 66

Great Pine portage, 110

Great Stone portage, 62–63

Great Whitewood portage, 99, 106

Groseilliers, sieur des: *1659* voyage of with Radisson, 33

Gunflint Lake, 22, 81, 88, 92

Gunflint Trail, 28

Handle of Sand (l'Anse de Sable, Lake Saganaga): Henry the younger on, 83

Harmon, Daniel, 44

Hat Point (Pointe aux Chapeaux), 28, 32, 35

Hauteur des Terres. *See* Height of Land; North Lake

Height of Land, 22; portage, 79–81, 88–89; continental divide, 81

Henry, Alexander, the elder, 34; traders at Grand Portage, 42; brief sketch, 45; French post on Lake Saganaga, 84–85

Henry, Alexander, the younger: Grand Portage trail, 50; cargo of canoe, 56; voyageurs at the Meadow, 60; narrows between Rove and Watab Lakes, 74; New Long portage, 75; Height of Land, 81; l'Anse de Sable (Lake Saganaga), 83; Indians making canoes, Basswood Lake, 107–108; Lac la Croix, 145; canoe-making on Sand Point Lake, 155

Hind, Henry, 9, 16, 133; encampment at Snake Falls (Namakan River), 16–18; description of Sturgeon Lake, 136; Namakan River, 157–158; Bare portage, 160

Hommes du nord, 37, 39, 123

Hopkins, Frances Ann, 149

Horse portage, 109–110

Hudson, Henry, 30

Hudson's Bay, 4, 5

Hudson's Bay Co.: organized, 5, 33; competition with North West Co., 5, 6; struggle with American Fur Co., 7; employs métis, 8; claims opposed by Canadian government, 9; mentioned, 32, 131, 155; blankets, 137

Hudson's Bay (York Factory) route to the Northwest: advantages over St. Lawrence–Lake Superior route, 5; replaces St. Lawrence–Lake Superior route, 7; mentioned, 10, 30, 33

Hunters' Island (Ile des Chasseurs): described, 94

Hurlburt, Rev. Thomas, 133

Huysche, Capt. Guy, 133; on the nam-

ing of Lac la Croix, 146; on canni-
balism on Loon Lake, 149

Indians: Pontiac uprising, 45; Park-
man on, 70–71; relics of warfare on
border, 111, 124, 127
Iron Lake, 123
Irving, Washington: on *coureurs de
bois*, 32; on annual meeting of North
West Co., 41; on French traders, 85
Isle portage, 135–136

Jacobs, Rev. Peter, 125–126, 133
Johnston, George, 155

Kaministikwia River, 33
Kaministikwia route: mentioned, 4, 6,
9, 131; replaced by Hudson's Bay
route, 7; used by Hudson's Bay Co.
officials, 8, 131; used by civilization's
vanguards, 8, 131–135; Canadian
Pacific Railway replaces, 8; assumes
importance as part of Dawson Road,
8; junction with Grand Portage route
in Lac la Croix, 22, 144–145; comparison with Grand Portage route,
22; La Vérendrye on, 33–34; redis-
covered by McKenzie, 79; boundary
dispute, 95; early use by French,
131; used by North West Co., 131
Kane, Paul, 133
Kennicott, Robert, 33; on galette on
Maligne River, 137–138; on lobstick
on Lac la Croix, 145
Kettle (Chaudière) Falls (outlet of
Namakan Lake), 156, 165
Kettle (Chaudière) Falls (outlet of
Rainy Lake), 161
Kettle portage, 161
King William's Narrows, 152, 153
Kipling, John: quoted on Maugenest
on Sturgeon Lake, 137
Knife Lake, 22, 98, 105
Knife portage, 98
Knife River, 98–99, 105–106

La Corne, Louis François de, 34
La France, Joseph, 34
La Jemeraye, sieur de, 33

La Vérendrye, Jean Baptiste, 33, 114;
brothers, 33
La Vérendrye, sieur de: on routes west
of Lake Superior, 33–34; sketch, 33–
34; uses Grand Portage route, 33; on
Grand Portage, 45; on Arrow Lake,
75; party massacred on Lake of the
Woods, 114; mentioned, 131, 161;
on Bourassa on Vermilion River,
153–154
Lac la Croix, 10, 22, 124–147
Lachine, 38
Lake of the Woods, 4, 34, 114, 154
Lesser Cherry portage, 67
Lewis and Clark, 8, 30
Little Basswood portage, 109–110
Little Knife portage, 98, 105
Little Muddy portage, 66
Little Stone portage, 111–112
Little Vermilion Lake, 151
Lobstick (Maypole): defined, 145
Long, Maj. Stephen, 132
Long portage, 66
Loon Lake, 147, 149
Loon portage, 149–150
Loon River, 22, 124, 147–151, 162–163
Lower Basswood Falls (Basswood
River), 111
Lower Lily Lake, 66
Lyed corn and grease, 37; Macdonell
on, 36; Mackenzie on, 60–61

Macdonell, John, 35, 99; on Grand
Portage, 35; on Fort Charlotte, 54;
on voyageur ceremony at Height of
Land, 80
McGillivray, William, 5
McKay, John, 6
Mackenzie, Sir Alexander, 10; on
Grand Portage, 39, 42; brief sketch,
46; Grand Portage trail, 49, 51–52;
lyed corn and grease, 60–61; *dé-
charge*, 62–63; New Long portage,
75; canoe incident on Rat Lake, 79;
Basswood Lake, 99; Picture Rock
(Crooked Lake), 113–114; furs
taken in Northwest, 148; Namakan
Lake, 156
McKenzie, Roderick: rediscovers Ka-

178

ministikwia route, 79; Henry the younger on, 108
McLoughlin, Dr. John, 143; on Crane Lake, 26, 154–155
McTavish, Simon, 5
Maligne River, 22, 124, 130, 131, 135, 136–144
Mangeurs du lard, 37, 39
Masson, Rev. William, 133
Master Pedlars. *See* North West Co.
Maugenest, Germain, 137
Meadow (Pigeon River), 60; Henry the younger on, 60; Thompson on, 60; Bigsby on, 60
Mesaiger, Father Charles, 33
Methye portage, 46
Métis (half-breeds): employed by the Hudson's Bay Co., 8
Millstone (Table) Rock (Crooked Lake): Thompson on, 115
Minnesota route to the Northwest: replaces York Factory–Fort Garry route, 10
Missionaries: Roman Catholic, 4, 33, 132–133; Protestant, 133
Missouri River, 4, 47, 161
Montreal, 4, 6, 7, 8, 22, 131
Montreal canoe, 38, 43
Monument portage, 94, 105
Moose Lake, 6, 8, 65, 66, 67–70
Moose portage, 64
Mount Rose, 28
Mountain Lake, 67–73
Mud portage, 149
Mutton Island (Lake Superior), 28, 39

Namakan Lake, 22, 156–165
Namakan Narrows, 155–156
Namakan River, 16–18, 156–160
Nantouagon. *See* Pigeon River
Nelson, George: incident on Pigeon River, 59–60
New Long portage, 22, 74–76, 77
Nipigon, Lake, 33
North canoe, 56–57, 123–124
North Fowl Lake, 64
North Lake, 81, 91–92
North West Co.: agents, 4, 40; organized, 5; Wallace on, 5; accomplishments, 5; competition with Hudson's

Bay Co., 5–7; posts in Quetico-Superior, 6; illegal posts in U.S., 6–7; union with Hudson's Bay Co., 7; route from Montreal, 22; uses Grand Portage, *1780–1804*, 34; clerks, 40; sketches of famous men, 45–47; changes rendezvous to Fort William, 80; interior posts and men, 123; weight of goods and number of men sent to the interior, 123–124; mentioned, 131, 132; Mackenzie on, 148; value of furs, 148–149. *See also* Voyageurs
Northmen. *See* Voyageurs
Norwood, Joseph: on cascades (Pigeon River), 55–56; on Crane Lake gorge, 152–153; on pictographs, Namakan Narrows, 156
Noyelles, sieur de, 34
Northwest Angle, 9

O'Leary, Peter, 135; on Sturgeon Lake, 136; on Dawson portage, 147
Orignal. *See* Moose Lake
Outardes. *See* North Fowl Lake
Ottertrack Lake, 96–98
Owen, David Dale. *See* Norwood, Joseph

Pays d'en haut: defined, 3
Palliser, Capt. John, 9, 133; report of expedition, 9; on Namakan River 159–160
Parkman, Francis: on Chippewa, 70–71
Partridge portage, 59
Pemmican, 6, 46, 60
Perches. *See* South Lake, 79
Pictographs: Crooked Lake, 113–115; Lac la Croix, 124, 125; Namakan Narrows, 155–156
Pièce: defined, 37
Pierres à Fusil. *See* Gunflint
Pigeon River, 29, 55–64
Pin décharge (Décharge des Epingles), 81
Pipe: defined, 145
Pointe du Mai, Lac la Croix, 144–145
Pond, Peter, 10, 34; brief sketch, 46; on voyageur custom, 38

Pontiac, Indian uprising, 4
Pork-eaters, 37, 39
Portaging, 112; Delafield on, 49–50
Posé: defined, 49
Port Arthur, 9
Potties. *See* XY Co.
Prairie portage, 99, 106
Prince Arthur's Landing, 9
Provencher, Rev. Joseph Norbert, 132

Quetico-Superior country, 3–8, 10, 30, 82, 100

Radisson, Pierre Esprit: formation of Hudson's Bay Co., 5; *1659* voyage of, 33; on *tripe de roche*, 124–125
Rainy Lake, 8, 10, 22, 39, 101–102, 123, 160, 161
Rainy Lake watershed: geology of lakes, 82
Rainy River, 4, 6, 8, 100, 161
Rat Lake, 79
Rat portage, 78
Rattlesnake portage, 17
Red River, 6, 9, 10, 132
Red River settlements, 5, 6, 9, 16, 132, 133
Richardson, Sir John, 133
Riel, Louis, 9
Riel rebellion, 9, 133
Road defined, 8
Rose Lake, 76, 78
Rove Lake, 73, 74
Rubbaboo, 125–126

Saganaga, Lake, 4, 22, 83–94
St. Lawrence–Lake Superior route to the Northwest, 3, 5, 30, 33; Ottawa River route from Montreal to Grand Portage, 38. *See also* Kaministikwia route, Grand portage route, St. Louis River route
St. Louis River, 33; route, 95, 152
Saint-Pierre, Jacques de, 34, 45
Ste. Anne, church of, 38
Sand Point Lake, 147, 151, 152, 154, 155
Saskatchewan River, 4, 45, 46
Sea Gull River, 82
Selkirk, Lord, 5, 6, 64; quoted, 63

Simpson, Frances, 132, 145, 157
Simpson, Sir George, 131, 132, 133, 146; on Maligne River, 139
Soldiers' portage, 156, 160
South Fowl Lake, 63, 64
South Lake, 79; portage, 79
Steinham, Rev. Henry, 133
Sturgeon Lake, 10, 22, 130, 131, 136, 137
Superior, Lake, 4, 9, 16, 27–28, 29, 33
Swamp Lake, 94
Swamp portage, 94, 104
Swiss de Meuron mercenaries, 6

Tabeau, Rev. Pierre Antoine, 131–132
Tanner, John, 67, 139; experiences at Grand Portage and Moose Lake, 67–70; shot on Maligne River, 140–144
Tanner's Lake, 139–140
Tar Point (Namakan Lake), 156, 157, 159
Thompson, David: geographer to Canadian boundary commission, 25; brief sketch, 46; Fort Charlotte, 57; the Meadow, 60; mentioned, 76; Prairie portage, 99; Crooked Lake, 114, 115; Namakan Lake, 160
Traineaux de glace, 101
Treaties: Treaty of Peace, *1783*, 7; Treaty of Ghent, *1814*, 25; Webster-Ashburton Treaty, *1842*, 95–96
Tripe de roche, 124–125
Twin Falls (Maligne River), 135
Twin Falls portage, 135–136

Upper Basswood Falls (Basswood River), 109–110
Upper Lily Lake, 66
U.S. Point (Basswood Lake), 108, 109

Vaseux. *See* Lower Lily Lake; Upper Lily Lake
Vermilion, Lake, 108, 152
Vermilion River, 25, 152, 153
Voyageur Island (Lake Saganaga), 83
Voyageurs: mentioned, 3, 8; Hind on, 17–18; described, 23–24; clay pipes, 29; northmen (hommes du nord), 37, 39, 123; pork-eaters (mangeurs

du lard), 37, 39; customs, 38, 39, 73, 80, 111; Mackenzie on, 39; engagements, 43; as sources of place names, 58; songs, 58–59, 147; duties and life at winter posts, 100; manner of portaging, 112; night encampment, 116

Wallace, W. Stewart: quoted, 5
Warrior Hill (Lac la Croix), 124
Watab Lake, 73, 74; portage, 73
Webster-Ashburton Treaty, 95–96

Wheelbarrow Falls (Basswood River), 111; portage, 111
Wilkins Bay (Lac la Croix), 147
Winnipeg, Lake, 34, 73, 161
Winnipeg River, 161
Wolseley, Col. Garnet, 9, 133, 139

XY Co.: organization, 40; mentioned, 46, 124; Mackenzie's relation, 46

York Factory route. *See* Hudson's Bay route

J. ARNOLD BOLZ was born in Elgin, Illinois, in 1918. He met his wife Belva at Crane Lake, Minnesota, on a canoe trip in the 1930s, and they explored the canoe country together until their deaths in 1991. He was an accomplished nature photographer whose work was published in *Wilderness Days,* by Sigurd F. Olson, and *The Boundary Waters Wilderness Ecosystem,* by Miron Heinselman. Bolz was active in the fight for wilderness preservation and in the formation of Voyageurs National Park and the Boundary Waters Canoe Area Wilderness.